"This book isn't just about pretzels. From the simple life of an Amish family, living in community, through tragedy, betrayal, violation, and finally, reconciliation, Anne Beiler's story will grab you and never let you go. It is, after all, a story of forgiveness, hope, and promise. It is about what Love can do."

Gloria Gaither
Author, Lyricist, Speaker

"In the pages of this book you will experience the highs and lows of the life of Anne 'Auntie Anne' Beiler. It will inspire you to face your obstacles—personal, professional, spiritual—and to live the biblical principal '. . . with God, all things are possible' (Matt. 19:26). It is a story of courage and faith."

Don M. "Bubba" Cathy
Sr. VP for Chick-fil-A

"Anne's extremely candid sharing of the highs and lows in her personal journey are a powerful real life story that will capture your attention, stir your emotions, and cause you to stop and reexamine your own life. It is a story of family love, support, and encouragement that overcomes grief, guilt, depression, and hopelessness. It is a story of forgiveness, God's grace, and redemption.

Don Soderquist
Retired Vice Chairman & COO of Wal-Mart Stores

"Anne Beiler traversed barren lands of emotional, relational, and financial disaster, and the journey prepared her for great achievements in each of the areas of her greatest challenges. Anne's story illustrates the overcoming strength that comes from faith, vision, and a commitment to serve. This amazing and uplifting narrative will touch the heart and motivate each reader to reach beyond failure to achieve full potential. I couldn't put it down until I read every page!"

Tom Wilson, Ph. D.
Superintendent, Life School, Dallas, Texas

"Anne Beiler is an inspirational and exceptional woman. From unimaginable tragedy to success in business, her story is filled with faith and optimism. Anne is a blessing to everyone who has the good fortune to know her by reading this book."

Ben Shanley
East Region Vice President, Coca-Cola FoodService

TWIST OF

Faith

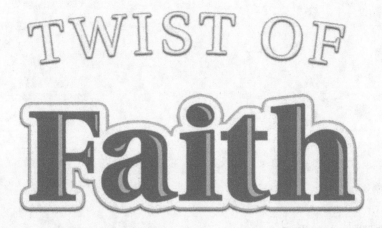

ANNE BEILER
WITH SHAWN SMUCKER

THOMAS NELSON
Since 1798

NASHVILLE   DALLAS   MEXICO CITY   RIO DE JANEIRO

Published in Nashville, Tennessee, by Thomas Nelson. Thomas Nelson is a registered trademark of Thomas Nelson, Inc.

Thomas Nelson, Inc., titles may be purchased in bulk for educational, business, fund-raising, or sales promotional use. For information, please e-mail SpecialMarkets@thomasnelson.com.

Scriture references marked NLT are taken from *The Holy Bible*, New Living Translation. © 1996. Used by permission of Tyndale House Publishers, Inc., Wheaton, Illinois, 60189. All rights reserved.

ISBN 978-1-59555-340-9 (tp)

Library of Congress Cataloging-in-Publication data

Beiler, Anne, 1949–
   Twist of faith / Anne Beiler with Shawn Smucker.
     p. cm.
   ISBN 978-0-7852-2323-8(hc)
    1. Beiler, Anne, 1949- 2. Women cooks--United States. 3. Auntie
Anne's Incorporated—History. 4. Amish—Social life and customs. 5.
Family—Psychological aspects. I. Smucker, Shawn. II. Title.
TX649.B446B463 2008
641.5092—dc22
[B]

2007052322

Printed in the United States of America

09 10 11 12 LSI 8 7 6 5 4 3 2 1

For Jonas, my dear husband,
and my daughters LaWonna and LaVale,

And to the memories of Angie, our sweet angel,
and my dad, whose presence was with me
as I wrote this book.

Contents

Contents

CHAPTER ONE

My Angie

I walked a mile with Pleasure / She chatted all the way
But left me none the wiser / For all she had to say
I walked a mile with Sorrow / And ne'er a word said she
But, oh, the things I learned from her / When Sorrow walked with me!

—ROBERT BROWNING HAMILTON

And just like that, the journey ended. I had covered so much ground during those years, walked so many miles. I went through the darkness, at times unsure if I would make it. I also walked the mountaintops and accomplished more than I ever dreamed possible. Do journeys always seem to end so abruptly? This one did. One moment I was caught up in running a business, and the next moment suddenly we were walking away from it: after seventeen years and building over eight hundred locations, we decided to sell Auntie Anne's Soft Pretzels.

One moment represented the climax of that journey's end: my husband, Jonas, and I sat alone on a stage at the annual

Auntie Anne's convention, in front of nearly one thousand franchisees, corporate employees, and family members. I felt as though nearly everyone fit into the last category: family. In many ways those franchisees and employees served as family through the years. We spent holidays with them, attended their weddings and their funerals, and sent congratulations on the arrival of children and grandchildren.

I desperately clung to Jonas's hand. He began his adult life as a mechanic by trade, something that fit into his true calling: fixing things. Initially this worked itself out in his life when he owned a body shop, beating old cars into shape. Eventually he channeled his efforts into counseling, tuning the engines of broken lives, making them purr again. I think when most people meet him, they see his serious side, his compassion. What many people don't see is that really he's just a little boy, downright silly at times. Sitting beside me on the stage, he made me feel strong and capable.

Some of my oldest and dearest friends talked about when they first started with Auntie Anne's. Their stories about broken-down delivery vans and grand opening day disasters put all of us in hysterics. But they also told stories that made me cry, stories about the changing of fortunes, how Auntie Anne's altered their lives for good, forever.

Two of our first franchisees in the South told their story of wanting to open a location in spite of our hesitancies. "You're too far away," we told them. "We're not ready to incorporate a store that far away into our infant distribution system." Back in the early '90s, we struggled to keep up with the business, growing mostly in Pennsylvania, and we couldn't imagine expanding so many hundreds of miles away. We eventually resigned ourselves to their pleas, agreeing to meet them halfway between their hometown and the interstate with their delivery once a month. These days franchisees receive deliveries on their doorstep, once or even twice a week. But back then we sometimes had to do things the hard way if we wanted to grow.

As other franchisees spoke kind words, my eyes fought the glare of the spotlights to search the crowd. Stories flashed through my mind as I scanned those faces. Hundreds of success stories, rags-to-riches tales that warmed my heart. Some faces brought to mind difficult times, conflict, and disagreement, but that went with the territory. There's nothing like the combination of money, passion for a product, and competition to stir up disagreement. Then, through the searching beam, I saw Charlie Johnson.

I remember one of my first trips to California to meet Charlie, a new franchisee. He drove me around in his sports car, gave me a tour of his stores in San Francisco. He seemed so full of peace and compassion, a family man. I attended church with Charlie over Mother's Day weekend and got to know him, heard his story. I soon discovered where the connection I felt came from—he'd experienced the tragedy of losing someone close to him, just like I had. When I told him the story about my daughter Angela, tears welled up in his eyes.

"I'm so sorry you lost your daughter," he said that day, Mother's Day. He repeated the statement many times after that: "I'm so sorry you lost your Angela." Charlie somehow understood I never stopped thinking about her. Even before I got up on stage the final day of our convention, he approached me, said how happy he was for me, but the last thing he said echoed in my spirit: "I really think your success is somehow connected with Angie being in heaven. I think she's pulling some strings for you up there."

"I think you're right, Charlie. I think Angie played a huge part in all this. I've always thought . . ." But I couldn't continue. Just the thought of her, of Angie, well, I stood there shaking my head, unable to press words past the rising emotion.

A warm autumn day in September 1975, and I walked barefoot in the grass along the stone drive. My daughter LaWonna ran ahead of me, her thin four-year-old legs spinning toward my sister-in-law's house. LaWonna's brown hair danced. Nineteen-month-old Angie tried to keep up, her chubby bare feet and uncertain steps sending up dust. Shirl and her four children lived only a hundred yards or so down the lane, and LaWonna loved playing there with her cousins. As LaWonna dashed up to the door and knocked, Angie stopped halfway between us and looked back at me. Her little blue eyes, impatient, seemed to say, "Are you coming, Mama?" She smiled, then turned and ran.

We spent a lot of time with Shirl and her children, but on that particular morning something weighed heavily on my mind, something I hoped Shirl would understand. We sat at her kitchen table and talked over coffee while children's voices skipped to us through the open window.

"Shirl, I've been having these dreams," I said. "I keep thinking someone in our family is going to die." I looked down, afraid she might think me silly for believing in my dreams, or perhaps she might think I doubted God's ability to protect us. But when I looked up, her face seemed pale and drawn.

She leaned forward and whispered, "I've been having the same dreams, Anne."

✣

Sitting on the stage, looking through the crowd and remembering stories, listening to franchisees talk about the old days when Auntie Anne's first started: everything felt like a dream. But before I knew it, someone turned off the stage lights, and a rustling began around the edges of the crowd. I thought to myself, "That's it—it's all over, my last convention as owner of Auntie Anne's."

Not yet.

Through the darkness I could hear one of my favorite songs beginning, "Go Light Your World." The word LIGHT holds special significance for us at Auntie Anne's, an acronym signifying our statement of purpose: Lead by example, Invest in employees, Give freely, Honor God, and Treat all business contacts with respect.

My corporate employees lit candles all along the edge of the auditorium. The candlelight spilled along the front row, illuminated the faces of my two daughters, LaWonna and LaVale, and sent a shiver down my spine. I could feel Angie. Somehow I just knew she sat there with me. Then the gentle glow of candlelight began to spread.

✣

The light spread through the kitchen in our small trailer home on that Monday morning, September 8, 1975. My bare feet padded across the cold linoleum floor. I turned on the stove and began making breakfast. My journal entry from the day before reads:

> *Sunday evening we all went to church. My sisters and I didn't sing that night, so I was with Angie in the nursery all evening, which was unusual. She played so much with her cousin Quentin . . . Came home after the service and made some eggs and things to eat. Angie was quite a character that night. I finally put her to bed at 12:30. She fussed for a while and finally Jonas went in and told her to lay down, and she settled down and went to sleep about 1:00. Checked the girls before we went to sleep, and all was well.*

As eggs sizzled and bacon spattered, I heard a sound behind me—imagine my surprise, after a late night, to see Angie's cute little face smiling toward me. She wanted to help with breakfast.

Shortly after Angie woke, the house bustled with activity: a group of guys who spoke at our church and spent Sunday night at our house packed their belongings in our small living room, then joined us for breakfast. The morning practically over-flowed with life, laughter, happiness, and the growing noise of hungry men eating (knives and forks against plates) while Angie entertained them.

Before they left, we decided to pray. Jonas and I stood together, holding hands, while my daddy blessed the men before they left—Angie wedged her way in between Jonas and me, her tiny hands grasping ours. LaWonna had left a few moments ear-lier, dashing outside to play with her cousins.

Just as Daddy came to the end of his prayer, he paused, but instead of ending in a typical fashion, he said something strange: "And, Lord, if there is a tragedy today, help us to accept it. Amen."

Those words embarrassed me—how could Daddy pray about tragedies with the long drive these kind men had before them? Jonas and I kind of chuckled it off as another one of my father's eccentric moments. But those words would echo in my mind for the rest of my life; I'm sure I'll never forget them. Why didn't those words alert me to what was about to happen? Why didn't I do things differently that morning?

The next few moments passed in a whirlwind of activity and good-byes and men carrying large bags through the door. Jonas helped them pack all of their things into the car and drove out down the lane—he needed to take them back to our church, where their bus waited to whisk them off to the next church meeting a few hours away. I stood in the doorway, the autumn breeze fresh against my skin. I waved good-bye to them, watched the dust kick up behind Jonas's car. The leaves changed color during those weeks, and the lining trees along the main road just beyond our lane rattled their leaves together. As I turned to go back inside, Angie darted past me for freedom and her Grandma's house. I watched her move away, her pajamas blowing around her like a cloud as she passed through our yard. For one instant I thought, *I should call her back, dress her before she goes to her grandma's.* Instead, I walked into the kitchen—I would call Mom and let her know Angie would be there any moment. That split-second decision changed my life forever.

❖

The glow spread through the entire auditorium as hundreds of people lit their candles. The light shone unnaturally, threw shadows against the walls. The song, the radiance, the emotion overwhelmed my senses. I found myself on the verge of fainting, forced to lean on Jonas for support to prevent myself from collapsing under the weight of too much happiness, too much love, too much sadness, and too much grief.

Then came the most tranquil feeling of all: Angie was there. I mean, I could sense her walking through the auditorium. Not in a sad way or a scary way. I simply felt her there, felt her say two things to me.

First she said, "Look what I did for you, Mama!"

I could picture her giggling, laughing in that mischievous way that only she could. What would she look like now, at the age of thirty? What would her smile look like? Would her eyes remind people of mine or Jonas's? Would her blond hair have stayed blond?

The second thing she said was, "You did good, Mama. I always knew you could."

And then I remembered, she wasn't thirty. I pictured her nineteen-month-old form wandering the auditorium, peering down rows of seats, playing peekaboo with the person seated behind her, all the while her golden curls bouncing like new flowers in a strong spring breeze.

✦

I reached for the phone to call Mom's house and let her know Angie was on her way wearing her pajamas and that I would bring clothes for her after I got the kitchen cleaned up. I can still see my young hand reaching for that green phone: smooth, creaseless. Jonas and I were so innocent then, overjoyed to move into that sixty-foot double-wide trailer, our lives so simple. But on that day we arrived at the middle of a decade that became both the best and the worst of our lives. The first half of the 1970s presented us with five years of happy marriage and our first two daughters. The second half became a long walk through the kind of darkness I never even knew existed. It began on that day, September 8.

Screaming. That's all I remember. Horrendous screaming and then one single deep voice hollering: the voice of Daddy, but not the voice I usually heard when he played with the grandchildren, scaring them and chasing them around the barn. No, the voice that interrupted my hand reaching for the phone scared me because I had never heard that voice before, full of panic and a too-late despair. Then another round of screaming, this time women's voices.

No, I thought, *not Angie.*

"Not Angie," I said, pacing a circle in the kitchen, the phone hanging lifeless against the wall where I dropped it. "Not Angie, God, not Angie." As soon as I heard those screams, everything punched me in the gut: the dreams, the premonitions, the realization that everything I felt up to that point about a family member dying actually prepared me for this moment, this screaming nightmare of a moment. I pulled on my hair with both hands. "Dear God, no, not Angie."

I couldn't resist. I walked to the screen door, the front door still open, still letting in that autumn day's fresh breeze. My face pressed up against the wire mesh, my eyes not wanting to look. Running around the corner (that last precious corner where I saw Angie disappear) came Daddy. In his arms he cradled a tiny bundle wrapped in a child's pajamas.

Just as I felt Angie's presence at the convention the strongest, a rustling movement drew my attention down in front of the stage: a small group of employees and family, each of them part of the core group that helped me start the company, walked toward me with their candles lit. My brother-in-law Aaron was there with my sister Becky, my first employees. My mom walked toward the front, looking frail and making slow progress, but still so strong. Then I saw Fi with her dark brown hair and brown eyes, my youngest sister—she always played so much with our younger brothers when we were little, always wanted to play baseball with them or go ice skating or climb trees. When my two sisters are with me, I always feel like I can do just about anything.

The words of the song grew louder, and that small group of friends sang along with the music: *Take your candle, and go light your world.* I could hear Fi's clear voice ring out above all the rest. *If Angie was here*, I thought to myself, *she would be right there walking beside Fi.*

Even back then Fi loved to sing—we'd often hear her beautiful voice ringing clear and loud from wherever she worked. I think singing came naturally to her, but she also got a lot of practice as a little girl singing with me and my older sister, Becky, in bed, the lights off, everyone else quiet in the house. During the fall of 1975, Fi announced her engagement, the last of us three sisters to marry, and she wanted Angie to be her flower girl.

Only twenty-two years old on that day of Angie's accident, Fi worked hard for my Daddy's masonry business, scooping sand into the mixer with a shovel. Soon Fi and Ruth, my sister-in-law, worked through half of the pile of sand, so Fi ran into the neighboring barn for the Bobcat tractor.

Fi knew the grandchildren could be anywhere, so she always took her time backing out. Glancing over her shoulder, she checked to make sure the driveway was clear. Then she backed out and pulled into the barn, ramming the sand forward. She backed again, always checking, always looking.

The next time she looked over her shoulder, she saw Daddy waving his hands frantically and running toward the back of the Bobcat. Out of the corner of her eye, she saw a tiny body lying limp where the Bobcat's wheels rolled just moments before.

My Angie.

Daddy arrived at the back of the Bobcat, still waving his arms, still yelling, "Stop! Stop!" as he bent over to scoop up her body dressed in pajamas. For years Fi and I spoke of this moment in hushed whispers, just the two of us. I remember more than once Daddy happened to interrupt us discussing the accident. He wanted to talk about it, to tell us what he saw and experienced, but we never let him do it. "No, no," we'd say, "don't talk like that, Daddy," and we'd change the subject. Ours was a private grief, and neither one of us could bear the thought of hearing the details of those last moments. Now his body sleeps in the ground beside Angie's, and I feel horrible for never listening to him, never letting him purge himself of the horrible scene he must have witnessed.

Fi accidentally backed over Angie, nineteen-month-old Angie with the sweet smile and golden curls, and she watched Daddy run off toward my house, carrying the small bundle. Fi knew she was dead.

"I believe she's dead," Daddy choked out in a hoarse voice again and again as he came around the corner of the barn toward where I stood frozen in the frame of our front door. His mouth trembled with emotion. "I believe she's dead. I believe she's dead." I wouldn't take her, so he laid her down on the grass at my feet. She lay motionless and limp, but perfect. Not a drop of blood. Somehow I knew she didn't have a chance.

So I ran.

Up and down the sidewalk, in circles, then back and forth again, screaming and pulling my hair. I circled around again and stopped in front of Daddy. I wanted to run away. Just run down the road and through the fields and up into the hills, but I couldn't leave without Angie.

I picked her up. Children grow, and we tend to emphasize how big they're getting, but when I picked Angie up, I realized just how light she felt, how little her frame, how fragile her bones. The way she lay in my arms felt so natural, so normal: how could she be dead?

"Oh, Angie, no, Angie, oh no, God." A stream of words, and soon I ran again, this time with her. In the midst of the chaos one thought began growing in my mind: *I must get her to the clinic; they can help her at the clinic.* I sprinted down the lane toward Daddy's car, still carrying Angie, the stones cutting into my bare feet. I didn't even feel them.

✤

It took a long time for Jonas and I to make our way from the auditorium: days, centuries even. So many congratulations, so many farewells, so many tears and laughs and promises to stay in touch. It felt as though the end had arrived. I grieved the loss of the company with many of the same emotions with which I grieved the loss of Angie. And in many ways that last day of the convention served as the funeral: the tears, the farewells, the support from family and friends. But as I walked through the long halls, stopped again and again by another friend, another story, the smallest margin of doubt crept into my mind: *Did I make the right decision? Did I make a mistake in selling this company?*

Seemingly out of nowhere, one of our franchisees from California crossed the room and gave me a hug. Small talk. Smiles. Then he looked into my eyes and said something that comforted me:

"Anne, I have three words for you: it's all right."

❖

Thirty seconds later, a minute, two minutes, who knows how long, but eventually Fi found herself sitting all alone in an area of chest-high weeds alongside the barn while everyone else raced around in the chaos and tried to herd all the other children together. Her mind closed down as complete shock set in. She sat there, weeping, staring blindly at the back of Daddy's car as it tore out of the lane, sending stones and dust high in the air, carrying me and Daddy and Angie away. Fi remembers the moment the car turned out of the drive, the eerie silence left behind, and the way she put her feelings into a mason jar, screwed the lid on tight, and never opened it again.

Meanwhile, racing away in Daddy's car, I held Angie like a baby, glancing down at her small white face turning the lightest shade of blue. Besides that, she looked perfect, felt perfect. I held her close to help her fight the growing coldness spreading from the tips of her fingers and up her arms. Then I noticed a ruby red bead of blood coming from first one ear, then the other. Angie's nose began to bleed, just the slightest red sliver. I jerked my head up, stared through the front windshield, as if by not seeing Angie bleeding I could somehow make it not so.

Now, even thirty years later, I ask myself, *Why didn't I look at her in those last moments? Why did I look away from her precious face?*

Daddy drove quickly. Within five minutes we arrived at the clinic. I ran inside, once again paying no mind to the stones on my bare feet or the way I looked, disheveled and still in my housecoat, stained by Angie's bloody nose and ears. I walked straight up to the counter and gently laid Angie upon it as if she were only sleeping.

"I think she's gone," I whispered without a tear, my voice cracking only slightly.

The receptionist looked taken aback, then dashed around the counter and took Angie. I followed her as she walked quickly back to one of the examination rooms.

My eyes struggled to adjust to the room's dim light. The shadows pressed in. The doctor came and began examining my little girl, holding a stethoscope to her chest, looking in her ears and mouth. I wanted to tell him to be gentle—that she was just a little girl. Such a little girl, so small on that big table. Silence existed, nothing else. Once again I turned away, couldn't watch, only stared at the blinds on the window. The silence became unbearable. Finally I spun around, somehow still held back the emotion, and asked, "Is she gone?" willing him with all my might to say "No, she's almost gone, but we'll fight hard and save her. We can save her." *Please say that*, I thought, *please say you can save her.*

The doctor looked up at me with sad eyes, still leaning over Angie, his stethoscope dangling helplessly from his neck.

"There is nothing we can do."

He pulled the white sheet up over her face.

❖

Arriving in my hotel room at the convention that night, the sadness I felt about selling the company faded a bit. The positive aspects of the sale began sinking in: I would now have much more time to spend with my girls, my grandchildren, and Jonas; the challenges that came with running a family business were behind me; I would no longer have to worry about managing the expectations of 250 franchisees; and of course the most obvious outward plus: a bank account with more money than I had ever imagined.

I remembered being a little Amish-Mennonite girl, listening by my bedroom window one evening, eavesdropping. My aunts and uncles had come to the house because my parents weren't able to make ends meet. There were tears and voices talking in hushed tones. I don't know the details of the arrangements, but in the coming weeks relatives occasionally arrived bringing "extra" preserves, clothing their children had grown out of, and sometimes envelopes with money addressed to Mother or Daddy. During those times I realized we were poor. I began, even at that young age, to feel responsible, and I wanted to help my parents any way I could.

Now there we were, a million financial miles from that situation. Would all of this have happened if I would have called Angie back that day, if Daddy succeeded in getting Fi's attention, if Angie would have walked a different way, or if those men left our house ten seconds later? What a confusing feeling that can be sometimes, when I think about how I wouldn't be where I am today if Angie would have lived. What a difficult success, when so much of it seems hinged on the path my life took after that terrible day in 1975.

✣

Seconds, minutes, hours later: I can't remember much about the passage of time in the dim room where the doctor declared Angie dead, but at some point Jonas came into the room where Angie lay, still covered. I didn't dare pull the white sheet back. For a thousand years we stood there, Jonas holding me.

"We could pray for her, hon," I sobbed into his neck. "I think if we prayed hard enough, we could bring her back."

I believed it then, perhaps still do. I thought the strength of my emotion surely could have convinced God to bring my Angie back to me. Jonas's perfect response settled the matter. He didn't argue with me about the merits of prayer or the likelihood of bringing someone back from the dead. He didn't philosophize about the sheer number of people each day who lost someone and felt exactly like I did. He simply asked me a question.

"Anne," Jonas whispered into my hair, "do you really want to bring her back to this? This pain, this hurt?"

Looking down at the sheet that covered her broken and bleeding body, I knew the answer. We walked out the door, leaving her there under the white sheet, my little angel.

Jonas and I drove slowly back to the house. Nearly everyone we knew arrived before we did, our friends and family providing a much-needed refuge. When I walked into the house, my mother hugged me, crying.

She whispered into my ear, "Anne, Fi's not very good; she thinks you're mad at her." And I remember the guilt when I realized I never thought about Fi or how she felt. Never once during the whole ordeal did I take care of Fi—how awful she must have felt for driving over Angie! At that moment I decided, *Okay, I have to be strong for Fi.* I braced myself, walked slowly across the room through the crowd. Fi lay on the sofa, fetal position, clutching a pillow to her face. I could barely see her eyes peeking out from under the pillow—they looked wild and scared.

"Do you hate me?" Fi asked.

"Of course not."

"Can you ever forgive me?" Fi asked.

"It was an accident. Of course I forgive you."

Some may find it hard to believe, but forgiveness for Fi entered my heart immediately. I never felt angry or upset with Fi on the day Angie died, never since then. In fact, I think the fateful bond that joined Fi with Angie on September 8, 1975, somehow transferred to a bond between Fi and me.

The irony of the situation began sinking in over the coming days. I reflected in my journal:

Strange as it may seem, when we wrote our will, we had requested for Aunt Fi to take care of Angela, should any-thing happen to us . . . and the same day Angela's death was in the paper, Aunt Fi's engagement was in the paper. For some reason God had these two bound together . . .

The viewing came on Wednesday night, September 10, at 7:00. Jonas, LaWonna, and I went in before anyone else to see Angie for the first time in over two days. I already missed her terribly, and after entering Furman's Home for Funerals, I found myself pulling ahead, starting to run, but Jonas gently held my hand.

"Walk, Anne; walk to her."

The coffin seemed so small. Angie lay all in yellow, a rose freshly picked, the tiny body of an angel, completely at peace. But when I reached in to touch her, she felt too cold, and her golden hair lay lifeless. How could this be my Angie? How could it have come to this? How could God let something so terrible happen to someone so innocent?

Nearly seven hundred people came to see Angie that night. My friends from church grieved with me over the loss of such a precious child. Before her death, Angie's reputation had spread among the congregation as a child who smiled for everyone, waved her pudgy little fingers hello to anyone she made eye contact with. Now they all came to say thank you to Jonas and me for sharing our child with them, even if for such a short time.

Outside of the funeral home, Fi waited, unable at first to go in. When she finally entered, she could only glance at Angie's body for a moment. She clung to me for what seemed an eternity, the two of us joined together in an immeasurable sadness.

Finally the night ended. The final hug, the final condolence. Jonas, LaWonna, and I left after everyone else, and Mr. Furman walked us to the door. LaWonna became very upset. She didn't want to leave. A quivering frown sat below determined eyes. Finally I coaxed her troubles out of her.

"Momma, are we going to leave Angie here?"

"Yes, honey."

"Who's going to watch her?"

The funeral director bent down and looked into LaWonna's eyes.

"I'll watch her. We take very good care of little children. She won't be alone tonight."

Thursday morning came cloudy and gray. I prayed a simple prayer before the funeral: "Lord, if you really love me, please let the sun come out today." Perhaps a selfish prayer, but I felt that God could maybe give me a pretty day in return for my daughter. More than six hundred attended the funeral, with cars waiting up over the hill just to park at the church. The children's choir sang "This is the Day" and "When He Cometh."

As Angela's short little coffin drifted into the ground just outside of Maple Grove Mennonite Church, my five brothers sang, "Angie won't have to worry anymore."

I sat on the grass with Jonas and LaWonna, listening to the words of that song, and the sun crept out from behind the clouds. I looked up and silently said, *Thank you.*

We left her body there that day, turned our backs and returned to our small mobile home. Whenever we left the house, we drove past the spot where Angie lost her life. Every day, I heard the laughter of the other grandchildren floating up the lane. Every night, I would wait until Jonas went to bed before collapsing on the sofa, grief-filled sobs wracking my body.

Fi went back to work on Monday, shoveling sand in the barn and driving the Bobcat again and again over the very spot where Angie died, not because she wanted to, but simply because that is what we did then. We got on with things. We continued, usually in silence. So many things about the day of September 8 went unspoken: things between me and Jonas, or me and Daddy, or me and the rest of the family. And in those unhealthy silences grew bitterness and depression and guilt.

I tried to keep a brave face. My journal entries from that time sound persistent in their attempts at staying positive. But inside, behind the writing, I was scared of life, doubting my faith, and losing a sense of myself. I was only twenty-six at the time.

CHAPTER TWO

Into the Darkness

What would happen if one woman told the truth about her life?
The world would split open.

—Muriel Rukeyser

few days after the convention, I found myself at my daughter LaWonna's house. She had just moved back from California a few weeks earlier with her husband, Russ, and her children, Trinity and Ryan. I helped her unpack boxes and ready her new home. I couldn't believe she'd finally made the move—now my entire family lived within walking distance of my house. After Trinity's birth I had decided to make a priority of spending time with her, traveling to California every six to eight weeks even during the busiest times. Now her beautiful smile and tender spirit live just around the corner. Flashbacks come like jolts of electricity when I remember that LaWonna was Trinity's age, quiet and carefree, when Angie died.

My happiness over LaWonna's move home pretty much defined my life during those post-convention days. On the outside anyway. On the inside anxiety crept up: I didn't know what the future held or what my role in life would be. What would it feel like not to be Auntie Anne anymore? To cover the anxiety, I busied myself beyond belief: I ran like a marathon trainer; I worked around my house like a full-time maid; I drove from here to there and back again running errands; I set up times for coffee with friends, filled every remaining minute of my day to ensure I stayed busy and allowed no time for thinking. I even stayed up late at night reading, anything to keep my mind occupied.

❖

After Angie died, I felt useless. LaWonna had turned four the previous summer and required little maintenance, especially with all of the cousins around to play with. I found myself holding empty days, with no diaper changing or bottle feeding or baby carrying required. I spent most of the time crying on the sofa.

Jonas seemed to recover well from the accident. I thought he still looked sad, but I don't remember seeing him cry much about Angie, and our talks about the accident came few and far between. I began to feel embarrassed that I couldn't deal with her loss, began hiding my crying from everyone. Soon I slept on the sofa, not wanting Jonas to know I cried myself to sleep each night. An emotional wall began to rise between me and my husband.

I remember driving down the road with LaWonna one rainy day in December 1975. She was singing, and I was feeling sad, as usual. These were the days long before children sat in car seats or any of us wore seat belts regularly—LaWonna sat up front with me and edged over against my leg while I drove, put her arm around me, and looked up at my face.

"Shh, listen," she said with a serious voice. "Jesus is speaking to us."

"He is?" I asked her, playing along. "Hmm, what's he saying?"

"He said we're going to have a little baby sister this year."

My heart skipped a beat, and immediately I knew LaWonna was right. Not long after that Jonas and I discovered another baby was on the way.

During the January after Angie's death, I only went farther and farther down. I prayed for God to send me someone to talk to, perhaps another lady who could understand what I went through. Even discovering I was pregnant couldn't chase away the shadows that taunted me.

One Sunday my despair drove me to the altar at church, where I knelt and closed my eyes, asking God to help me make sense out of my emotions. I felt a strong hand on my shoulder. I looked up—my pastor stood there, concern etched on his face. He prayed with me. I wept. He knelt beside me there at the altar, his arm around me. For the first time in months, I felt comforted. Eventually we both stood up, I to return to my seat, he to climb the stairs back up to the pulpit. He hugged me one more time.

"I love you, Anne," he said kindly. His words didn't surprise me—our young church had grown close, and we always told each other, "I love you."

"I know you do. I love you, too," I said. Our congregation loved our pastor. It seems nearly impossible for me to describe the complete respect and admiration all of us at our church felt for him. His preaching seemed inspired, his pastoral care for our flock Christlike. Besides those things, everyone simply loved being with him—he made us feel at home.

"No, Anne," he said, looking into my eyes. "I love you in a special way. Please call me. We need to talk." That said, he walked back up to face the congregation.

Walking back to my seat, my mind spun. A special way? What did he mean by that? Did he love me that way because Angie died and as a part of the congregation he knew I needed a special love? I stood beside Jonas, finally feeling comforted but also confused. Something didn't seem right.

❖

I was excited that LaWonna had moved home from California with her family, and I got caught up in helping her unpack, but soon I realized it was getting late. Time to head home. Exercising came at the top of my New Year's resolutions, so after bundling up and walking outside, I prepared for the run home. The night sky shone clear, the air felt crisp, and my breath puffed out in foggy bursts. I rounded the corner into our housing development and mentally prepared for the long hill ahead.

Over halfway up I noticed headlights coming down toward me. No through roads crossed our development, so very few cars drove down that hill. I heard the gravel crunching and couldn't tell if the driver saw me running, so I stepped over into the snowy shoulder as the vehicle passed.

As I stepped back up onto the road, I misjudged the ledge on the side and stepped right on the lip. I heard the sound of a small twig cracking, then a searing pain shot up my leg. Soon I realized I hadn't stepped on a twig—something had snapped in my foot. I fell to the ground at the side of the road, clutching my foot in agony, angry at myself for not bringing my cell phone, wondering how in the world I could make it home.

❖

I told Jonas our pastor offered to meet with me to talk about Angie. He seemed fine with the idea—we respected our pastor and felt that if he thought I needed counseling, well, then it probably made sense. But I didn't tell Jonas what Pastor said to me at the altar that day. It was the first of many secrets.

"No, Anne, I love you in a special way."

I drove up through the woods to our church. The trees stood bleak on that winter day, looking cold and very much like stakes driven into the earth. The parking lot sat empty save two or three cars; after all, it was only a weekday. Entering my pastor's office seemed strange—I'd never gone for counseling before that and felt needy and weak that someone else had to take time out of his busy schedule to walk me through my problems simply because I couldn't deal with them on my own. I knocked on the thick wooden door.

"Come in, Anne," he said.

I immediately felt safe just going inside his office. Pastor walked to me from behind his desk and hugged me for a long time while I cried. He motioned towards a seat, and I felt so comforted in that chair across from him. His eyes looked concerned for me. He asked me so many questions. We talked for an hour or two. I couldn't believe how good it felt to talk about Angie, about the day she died, about how I felt. I wondered why I hadn't thought of meeting with Pastor before and thought to myself, *This must be God's way of answering my prayer about having someone to talk to.*

When the time came for me to leave, he walked me to the door. Nothing could have prepared me for what happened next: Pastor gave me another long hug, but this time when I looked up to thank him, he kissed me square on the mouth, a kiss he held in place for what seemed an awkward eternity. Finally he pulled away and said, "It's obvious to me, Anne, that you have needs in your life that cannot be met by Jonas. But I can meet them."

I nodded dumbly, not knowing what else to do. Somehow I ended up outside feeling very guilty and confused. Everything seemed cast in doubt—*Why would my pastor do that? I only wanted to talk about Angie. And why would he say those things to me?* As I fled to my car, only one thing seemed certain in my mind: I could never tell Jonas about what had just happened; he would never believe me.

✦

I sat in the cold, trying to figure out what to do about my foot. I hoped to get a ride from someone driving up the hill; after all, my house sat only a few hundred yards away. But no cars came by. Eventually I stood up. *One step at a time,* I told myself. *One step at a time.*

I could place hardly any weight on the damaged foot, but I began making progress. After fifteen, twenty, thirty minutes finally I arrived at the front door. The door stayed put, locked. I rang the bell and heard someone coming to answer.

"Anne, what's wrong?" Jonas said, looking perplexed as he opened the door.

I practically whimpered. "I hurt my foot. Please carry me."

Jonas picked me up and carried me gently through the

house to the sofa. He placed me there, propped my foot up on pillows, and got me something to drink. He gently took off my shoe and sock—the pain split my leg in two.

"Just cut it off," I moaned, trying to joke away the pain but nearly serious in my request.

Finally there it rested, my naked foot, bruised and swelling.

I met with Pastor quite often, usually at restaurants over a cup of coffee. While I felt uncomfortable after our first session, I desperately needed the time to talk about Angie, to work through my hurt, and Pastor seemed one of the few people in my life willing to just sit there and listen. *Maybe I imagined things,* I told myself. *Maybe he didn't do anything inappropriate.* After all, everything else about our meetings seemed so out in the open. I found myself reasoning everything away in order to spend time with someone who comforted me.

When I told Pastor at one of our meetings early in 1976 that I was pregnant, he became furious. He thought the whole idea of getting pregnant so soon after Angie's death was ridiculous and selfish. I never told him, but I felt happy about that little life growing inside of me. It hurt me deeply that he wasn't happy for me, but instead of questioning his motives, I questioned my own, wondering if getting pregnant so soon after Angie's death was the right thing to do.

Three months passed since our first meeting. One day Pastor asked me to meet him farther away than usual at the next town down the highway. We met in a diner and shared discussion over coffee. Then he said he needed to drive me somewhere. We drove a few miles away to a hotel, one of those single-story seedy-looking places you find a lot these days in between small towns. He asked me to follow him. I grunted as I climbed out of the car—my daughter LaVale (although I didn't know she was a girl at the time) was growing inside of me, and the added weight had begun making it difficult to get around.

I followed him into one of the rooms, feeling increasingly uneasy and confused. The door slammed behind me. Light filtered in around the curtain edges, but besides that the room was completely dark.

I sat in the doctor's office, the x-rays of my foot shining on the wall. The doctor explained to me why I didn't need a cast, why an air cast worked just as well in my case, why I needed to rest my foot as much as possible.

"But it's been a couple of weeks, Doc," I said, feeling discouraged. "Why does it still feel so tender? When will I be able to run again?"

He chuckled.

"Some things take a long time to heal," he said. "Some breaks stay tender for longer than we want them to. And you," he said with a mischievous look in his eye, "are not a young pup anymore."

"I know, Doc, I know. But right now it feels like I'll never be the same again."

"I know, Mrs. Beiler," he said politely. "You know, it would have healed a lot faster if you would have come in right after you hurt it. But you waited, what, two days? Hobbling around all that time on a broken foot? You did some extra damage by not coming in right away. But don't worry—now that you've come for help, you'll be fine. It'll heal. It just takes time."

✦

When Angie died, I thought I knew despair, but lying there on the bed in that dark motel room, I realized despair takes many forms, contains many different layers. Just when I thought I'd found the center of my despair with Angie's death, its rotten core split open, revealing hidden depths.

"No one's ever going to believe you," he said, sitting beside me in the car. "You know that, don't you?"

I thought he was probably right: who would believe me? He was the well-respected pastor of a loving congregation, I the obviously unstable woman who lost a child less than a year ago.

I know there were choices I could have made differently that day. Some people may wonder why I kept meeting with him, why I got in the car with him, why I agreed to go into the hotel room. I've asked myself those questions hundreds of times, and it's difficult to give an answer that makes sense. What I can say is that I completely trusted my pastor and that, at the time, he was the only person who cared enough to listen to my sadness. I was broken, grieving, and extremely vulnerable. I trusted him completely. It's what can happen when people in that position abuse their power—they can lead people down roads they never would have gone down on their own. Many years later I discovered this is called "abuse of spiritual power."

Sitting in that car, I thought to myself, *What just happened? Why did I let that happen?* I was so emotionally broken at that point, I felt I was beyond repair. From that moment on, heavy chains of guilt and self-loathing entwined themselves around me, and when I resolved to tell no one, I locked those chains firmly on myself. Telling the truth about what happened was the key to freedom, but I quickly tossed it aside, didn't even allow myself to look at that key for over six years.

CHAPTER THREE

A Homecoming

Make all you can. Save all you can. Give all you can.

—JOHN WESLEY

Photographs. Look at those pictures of times gone by and you are suddenly transported to that very spot, that very moment. When I look at pictures of myself from the early eighties (and there are few—I avoided cameras like a mouse hiding from a cat), there is the usual chuckle at the styles and haircuts of the day. But there's also something else I see, something others might quickly skim over: my eyes.

There's one in particular I noticed the other day, a picture taken during one of Jonas's family gatherings, where everyone else is eating around the table while I lean up against the kitchen counter, finishing my plate. I'm not sure who took the picture, but they caught me in midbite, raising the fork to my mouth. I'm wearing a maroon outfit with a black belt. My hair is just beginning to show hints of gray. Caught unawares by the mystery photographer, I was unable to put on the usual smile and appearance of cheer, and my eyes unveil the true state of my spirit: no spark, lifeless, fatigued, wishing those days would end.

❖

Imagine walking along through a beautiful field, admiring the wildlife and the flowers and a blue sky that almost lifts you off the ground. The smell of honeysuckle and the sound of birds singing. Then imagine suddenly falling into a pit so deep that the sky is nothing more than a pinpoint of light and the only sound you can hear is the rigid silence of the earth. Imagine being badly injured from the fall and barely able to crawl forward, but soon you see that even crawling is useless—the pit is too deep and all sides rise in walls, sheer cliffs. There is no way out. You lie down, giving in, prepared to die. Imagine lying there for six years.

But then imagine a sudden deliverance, waking to the morning light, the feel of grass under your bare feet and the smell of spring, the hint of freedom. From 1976 to 1982 I lay at the bottom of that pit, thinking the only thing that could save me was death. I wanted to die! But then, suddenly, I found a way out, discovered a way to the outside world. I was rescued.

❖

The year was 1986, and I sat in a warm bubble bath in Texas, reflecting on my life. Somehow, happiness had returned to me after Angie's death, six long years of abuse of power and trust by my pastor, the splitting of our church, and the division of our extended family. I'll tell the story of those ten years from

1976 to 1986 at a later time, but for now it's enough to say that I sat in the bath feeling completely at peace. My marriage felt restored, and Jonas and I experienced a newfound faith in God and church. Our family lived together in harmony. In the mornings, after the girls left for school, I would often retreat to the comfort of a hot bath. Sitting there on that particular morning, all alone and completely relaxed, I found myself in a mental conversation with God.

"Lord, this is really nice. I love this house. I love the last three years we've spent recuperating here. I feel like a good mom again. There's peace in our family, and Jonas and I get along so well.

"But is this all there is? It seems there must be more to life than this—to be honest, I'm getting kind of bored."

I stared at the ceiling, the bubbles fizzing around me as they popped, the warm water massaging my muscles. I thought about the mechanic shop that Jonas ran and his newfound desire to provide counseling for couples who were going through struggles like we went through. After all, good counseling got us through, and we both felt the hope that someday we might provide the same support for others.

"There must be more to life than just coasting by on peace and happiness. There must be a greater purpose."

Looking back, I realize now that God used those years in Texas to begin showing us that our purpose would be to give financially to people and ministries in need. On one particular Sunday, Jonas and I sat in our church listening to a speaker talk about tithing. Jonas and I always gave 10 percent of what we made to the church—we both felt that was the right thing to do. But on that particular day the speaker said something we could both relate to: if you don't feel that you are making what you're worth, perhaps you should try giving 10 percent, not on what you are actually making, but on what you feel you *should* be making, and trust that God will help you reach that new income level.

Jonas and I laughed to each other as we talked about the sermon on the way home, but there was a serious side as well: we were always so tight on money, living paycheck to paycheck. Yet Jonas worked very hard and was the best mechanic and auto body repairman in the area: I knew he was worth much more than what we were bringing in.

"So what do you think you're worth?" I asked Jonas. At that time he made around $250 per week.

"I think I'm worth at least $500 per week," he said with a smile.

Right there we decided to start giving $50 a week instead of $25 and to trust that God would send in the money we needed.

Two weeks later we were still giving the higher amount but knew we wouldn't be able to for much longer. In those days it was common practice for Jonas to receive short-term bank loans to cover the money he needed at his business for parts, just until he received payment. In order to cover the increased giving, we had to dip into these advance payments. At that time we spent about $25 per week on groceries, and the increased giving definitely affected us. Then a man came to Jonas's body shop looking for some help. He also ran a body shop and needed another employee. He needed the work done fast and was willing to take Jonas on full-time while still allowing Jonas to do his own work on the side.

"If you decide to come work for me," the man said, "I'll pay you $500 a week."

Amazing! Yet sitting there in the tub, I was still too close to that event to see the larger significance it held. As the steam rose around me, I whispered quietly to God, "I'm willing to do whatever, I mean *whatever*, you want me to do. I don't know what it is, but I'm willing. You've given me so much, restored so much of my life that I thought would never heal. Let me give back, if possible."

❖

I didn't get an answer right there in the bathtub, but during the next few weeks something began stirring inside of Jonas and me, a feeling of restlessness, as if the time had come to move on. Then came a trip up north, back to where we both grew up in Lancaster County, Pennsylvania, and during the long drive I couldn't help but feel our path must be leading us back there again. After the trip, we returned to Texas and I remember sitting down at the kitchen table with Jonas. I told him I had the strangest notion during the drive that maybe we should move home to Pennsylvania. Jonas looked at me with a smile and said he felt the same thing.

Just the thought of returning to Lancaster filled me with so many conflicting emotions. On the one hand I felt almost giddy with excitement at the thought of going home to those old familiar hills and fields, favorite haunts, old friends, and especially family. Yet Lancaster County still held so many other, more painful, associations: Angie's death only ten years earlier, the dividing of our church which once seemed so close. What would people think of me? My hometown is a small, tightly knit community, and by then it seemed that everyone knew everything about my life. God restored so much, but could he bring back all of our old friends with whom we parted ways so painfully? Still, I remembered the commitment I made to God, that I would do whatever he asked us to do, and both Jonas and I felt God was asking us to move home.

Finally, after many late-night discussions in bed and long days of thinking over our options, Jonas and I made the decision: we would move back to Pennsylvania. Now we just had to tell our girls.

Jonas and I decided to tell the girls about moving north over dinner. LaWonna, fifteen, and LaVale, ten, sat across from us: LaWonna's eyes and hair were a deep brown, and in those days she carried around with her the typical teenage confusion of still depending on us but wanting complete independence; LaVale's hair was lighter and her eyes green, and at ten she still retained more little-girl traits than her older sister. But she always had a lively spark in her eye that reminded me her teenage years were right around the corner.

Jonas spoke first.

"Girls, your mother and I have something to tell you."

A slight pause, and both girls looked at us, their eyes full of concern.

"We've decided to move back to Pennsylvania."

The four of us sat there in the Texas heat, completely silent. It took only a moment for the shock to pass.

"I'm not moving to Pennsylvania," LaWonna said with determination in her voice while rolling her chair away from the kitchen table. "I can't believe you would even think of it. You just want me to leave all my friends?" She ran upstairs, crying, and slammed the bedroom door behind her. At first LaVale just sat there staring at her plate, but then she too rose and slowly walked up the stairs, more likely to try to console her sister than as any kind of protest. LaVale's mission in life has always been to preserve peace in the family, something she has been doing since before she was born when just the promise of her birth helped ease the pain of Angie's passing. Jonas and I sat there, a little surprised by the forcefulness of LaWonna's response. I didn't think she would take the news so hard.

For the next few days, life became rather difficult around the house as the thought of moving north settled like a gray cloud over all of us. What were we supposed to do? Our family had finally reached a place of peace, only for the idea of moving to begin splitting us again. Finally Jonas called a family meeting and made an announcement that surprised us all.

"We are not going to move to Pennsylvania until we all feel that it's okay, that it's the right thing to do. So that's it. You girls just tell us when you're ready to move." And that was that: Jonas and I waited. Well, it's not entirely true to say that the only thing we did was wait: we also prayed, every day, that if it truly was God's will for us to move north, the girls would have a change of heart.

We spent Christmas of '86 in Pennsylvania with our family and enjoyed ourselves. The twenty-four-hour drive home felt longer that year, although I'm not sure why—perhaps I waited for one of the girls to drop the revelation that finally the time had come to move. But there was no such conversation, just miles and miles of wondering. Eventually we settled back into normal life, and 1987 got off to a good start. I mentally prepared for another good year in Texas.

One day, while I washed dishes in the kitchen, LaWonna

came up behind me and stood by the table. She started talking to me, just standing there and going on about different things, which seemed kind of strange. Then, I guess after she gathered enough courage, she kind of blurted out something like, "Mom, I know you're not going to believe this, but I really think God wants us to move to Pennsylvania."

I turned and stared at her, completely shocked. Her face held one of the most sheepish looks I've ever seen.

"Are you just saying that, LaWonna?"

"No, I really want to move to Pennsylvania."

LaWonna's decision to obey God affected our lives immensely. Her courage allowed our entire family to begin a new adventure. Without it, we could all still be living in Texas, Jonas working long hours in a body shop. I might be happily raising grandchildren, never knowing what might have been. There would be more defining moments over the coming months and years that dramatically altered the path my life was on and in the end would bring about Auntie Anne's Soft Pretzels.

*

There's a photo of our street the day before we left. How I miss that street, those familiar houses, the peaceful feeling of hope, desperately hoping that the worst times had vanished behind us forever! Our house is in the far left-hand side of the picture. In front of our driveway Jonas and Aaron (my sister Becky's husband) put the finishing touches on their creation: the "Brown Cow" (a two-tone brown passenger van) holding one of our motorcycles on a custom-made hitch and towing a trailer carrying a vehicle owned by one of our three families. The front light is on, dusk is settling in, and the street is quiet as most of the neighborhood children are inside preparing for bed.

❖

The morning after that photograph was taken, an eighteen-wheeler parked outside of our home. The morning sun had only just begun to shine, but already the summer heat shimmered up off the pavement in lazy waves. The six of us walked out the front door and down the sidewalk to the truck: me, my two sisters, and our husbands were together and ready to load up for our move home. In the end, all three of our families decided that returning to Pennsylvania was the right thing to do, and what better way to make the long move home than together.

Our friend drove trucks for a living and said he would drive our stuff from Texas to Pennsylvania. He dropped out of the truck and came around to greet us. We all felt very happy to see him, but also excited and nervous about the move.

As we loaded the truck, he went inside to take a nap in preparation for the long drive north. We began the long task of moving box after box after box, sofas and televisions and tables and chairs, all the belongings of three entire families.

We all decided that Jonas and I should pack our stuff first, toward the front of the truck, since we didn't have a plan for where to stay once we arrived. There we were, packing up my favorite house, leaving friends we loved, and moving over sixteen hundred miles, to a place that on one hand felt so familiar, and on the other hand so unknown. Aaron and my sister Becky had a place to live; Mike and Fi planned on staying with Mom in her basement for a little while until they found something;

we had nowhere to go! Literally, we did not know where we were going to put our furniture! We went ahead, knowing that something would open up for us. Through all of the excitement, a small part of me still wondered, *What have we done? Is this the right thing?*

Eventually we finished packing the truck. One of the men jumped up on the tailgate and slammed the door, latching it tight. And that was that: the house sat empty, everything we owned in what then seemed a pretty small space. First the six of us stood there, an eerie silence coming from the house. Then we walked quietly inside for a short rest before the long drive and a final cup of coffee.

"I can't believe we're leaving," one of my sisters said, her voice part enthusiasm, part apprehension.

"I know," I said, shaking my head and thinking to myself, *I love this place; I love this house. Why are we doing this? Why did I take that bubble bath? Why did I tell God I would do anything he wanted?* I was feeling like LaWonna when she first found out about our plan to move north, and part of me wanted to yell at God, "I'm not moving anywhere!" and open the back of the truck and just start unpacking.

The coffee was extra hot, just how I like it, and we all drank slowly, savoring our last moments in Texas—we all knew we would need the caffeine for the long drive ahead. Our kids ran around, full of excitement, ready to get the caravan moving, ready for the adventure. Just then our friend came walking up to us. *Strange,* I thought to myself. *What's wrong?* As he got closer, I saw that he was crying and visibly shaken.

He looked at Jonas and me with one of the most serious looks I've ever seen.

"You may not believe what God just told me, but this is what he said: he will restore every broken relationship, he will give back to you more than you ever had before, he has a plan for you that you don't know about yet, but he will show it to you."

Then he stopped and looked down, shaking his head as if he couldn't believe what he was about to say.

"I just see so much for you guys. And it's not just spiritual blessing. It's, well, you think this house is beautiful? And don't get me wrong, it is. But I see God giving you things you wouldn't believe: I see houses, I see land, I see cars, I see, I just see all that stuff.

"God is going to give it all to you. And you're going to start some sort of a business. I don't know exactly what kind, but that's the key. And it's going to happen within the first year of your arrival in Pennsylvania."

When he began telling us about what God had told him, we just sat and listened, feeling the weight of the moment. But when he added that part at the end about land and cars and houses, it struck me as so impossible that the only natural response was to laugh: not a laugh of happiness or even amusement, but one of total disbelief.

"Thanks a lot," I said with a voice full of doubt. "Yeah, thanks. I believe that one."

Everything we owned was in that truck! Couldn't he understand that? I was thirty-nine years old without life insurance policies or a plan for retirement. In the way of cash, after taking out the money we would need for gas and meals on our journey, we had an astronomical $25 left! $25! Yet there stood our friend talking about houses and land! Didn't he know we had nowhere to stay? We couldn't even sell our house and in the end gave it back to the bank. And cars? Didn't he see the old brown Toyota Celica station wagon parked in front of his tractor trailer?

So where would all this money come from? Jonas was a mechanic, an amazing mechanic, but the amount he could make working on cars seemed rather limited. How could a mechanic's business bring about all this stuff he talked about? We wanted to counsel people, but not for money. In fact, we dreamed about providing that for free to those who needed it. But providing free counseling doesn't fatten up the checking account.

I couldn't help but poke fun at our friend's prophecy.

"Yeah, okay, whatever you say."

But my response brought about a grave change in the look on his face. He shook his head with disappointment.

"Okay, fine," he said with resignation in his voice. "There was more, but I'm not telling you any of it."

"Fine by me," I said, the laughter still in my voice.

I brushed his words aside and for a while forgot them completely, but the day was just around the corner when I would think of that prophecy and shake my head in amazement.

The next few pages in my photo album are full of those traveling moments: children asleep, surrounded by suitcases and makeshift beds; profile shots of tired drivers hypnotized by mile after endless mile of roads and trees and sky; rest-stop pictures and tired mornings eating in the same restaurants.

Just making our way out of Texas took an eternity. Then we drove through Arkansas and into Tennessee. Long hours, some of which were loud and fun as we all chattered over the two-way radios installed in a few of the vehicles. But more than a few of those long hours passed full of quiet contemplation, Jonas driving while I stared out the window, watching the grass, the trees, the miles flash by. We had come so far, not just on that trip, but in life, and I couldn't help but wonder where we were headed.

As we came into Nashville, the sky darkened. We all talked over the radios, shouting to each other with each bright flash of lightning, counting the seconds separating the bolts from our cars. The girls rode in the car ahead of us. Suddenly the storm's intensity increased.

Rain came down in sheets to the point where we couldn't even see the car in which LaWonna and LaVale rode. The wind shook our car back and forth. The lightning flashed. After a few minutes of attempting to drive through the torrent, Jonas pulled over to the side of the road and stopped as I attempted to reach the girls on the radio.

"LaWonna? LaVale?" I had to shout just to raise my voice over the pounding sound of the rain on the roof of our car.

But all that came back through the receiver was an intense crackling.

"Fi? Becky?"

Still no answer, but all we could do was sit there in the storm and wait for it to pass. Jonas held my hand—he could tell that worry stood on the verge of panic as I thought about my girls out there in the storm. I wanted to get out of the car and run through the rain until I found them.

Then, in what seemed an instant, everything went sunny and quiet.

"Look!" Jonas said in a voice that sounded like a shout in the newfound silence.

In front of us the storm raged on, the trees bending one way.

Then Jonas told me to look through the back window. The trees behind us bent in the opposite direction. We were in the middle of the storm. I still couldn't see the girls anywhere, but the feeling of peace was so intense right in that spot that I already felt the panic fading away.

The back of the storm overtook us, and again came the feeling of fear, the feeling of being submerged. Gradually the rain died away and we took to the road once more. Soon the radios worked and all of us connected, our voices full of relief to find everyone okay. But I couldn't shake the memory of sitting in the middle of that thunderstorm. *Peace in the storm*, I thought to myself. *So that's what it feels like.*

One other event, a simple conversation actually, jumps out in my mind when I think about that journey north, and it happened shortly after we passed through the storm. Our caravan reassembled with Jonas and me still driving the brown van, just the two of us. As we approached the Tennessee border, we began talking more about our dream of providing counseling to couples. We weren't affiliated with any particular church, and my experience with Pastor still sat close in our rearview mirror, leaving a septic taste in my mouth when it came to church and pastors in general. Without a church or a pastor to come to us and say, "Will you be our counselors?" we weren't sure how to get involved. Yet we knew we could offer so much—our marriage had gone to hell and back, and we wanted to give that hope of recovery to others.

As we talked and became more excited at what we thought we could offer, Jonas started talking about building a center where families could come for all kinds of free counseling.

"What kind of counseling center are you talking about?" I asked.

"Well, a little bit like Dr. Dobbins has at EMERGE Ministries. A nice building with a lot of offices and meeting rooms."

At first I didn't say anything, but my eyebrows shot up in surprise.

"Whoa," I finally said, then slapped him on the knee with a laugh and continued. "So, honey, where do think you're going to get the money to do this?"

"Oh," he said, "I'm not worried about it. If God wants me to do it, then he'll provide the money."

"Well, let me say one thing clearly," I said. "If you want to build a big building and start a counseling center, I am never, *never* going to ask anyone for a dime. If God wants us to do this, then he will have to do something very big for us."

✦

Turn the page to another photo, this one taken from the passenger seat of an old Buick on the highway, the road stretching out in an endless line before us. I can see Aaron and Becky's gray truck loaded down, nearly dragging on the road, and the back of a trailer holding chairs, a table, and two motorcycles. The Celica races ahead, still carrying the words written in soap on the passenger-side window: "We messed with Texas . . . Penn or Bust!" In real life we cruised at 65 miles per hour, racing north, but in the photo all of the vehicles are frozen in time, waiting to drive under an overpass holding a huge green sign: "Welcome to Pennsylvania."

Turn the page and find another sign frozen in time, this one tied between Mother's garage roof and a tree, stretching over her driveway. Multicolored balloons the shape of giant hot dogs dangle down as we drive under it. Black and red lettering carefully written on brown paper spells out a message that still pushes tears into my eyes:

"WELL-COME on HOME!"

✦

There we sat—it didn't seem quite real. All of my brothers and sisters greeted us with their husbands and wives and children. The only one missing was my brother Chub, who decided not to make the move north with the rest of us—this was one of the most disappointing parts of our decision to return to Pennsylvania.

Still, I thought to myself, *this is it. This is home now.*

We unloaded Mike and Fi's things at Mom's house and eventually headed over to Aaron and Becky's to help them move into their home. As we unpacked the trailers and moved the boxes, my brother Jake pulled me aside.

"Where are you guys staying?" he asked me.

"We're not sure yet," I said.

"Well, you know I've got that mobile home that needs some fixing up. If you and Jonas don't mind doing some of the work around the place, you can stay there for free."

I talked to Jonas, and we decided to accept Jake's offer. We had a home.

The next few weeks passed quickly. Jonas did some mechanic work for friends and family and began counseling people in the community. It didn't take long for people to find out that we were offering free counseling for couples. I kept busy by running the girls here and there and everywhere, enrolling them in schools and taking them to their cousins' houses. But when it came to finding part-time work, I came up empty-handed.

I had worked as a waitress for numerous restaurants before we moved to Texas and naively thought that surely someone would remember what a good waitress I was and take me back. I went back to the restaurants I'd worked for but to no avail. They had already hired their summer help.

Coming away from one of them, I turned to Jonas.

"I just don't know what's wrong," I said in desperation. "All these people know me and know I'm a good waitress. Why don't they hire me?" I felt I had exhausted all of my options and gave in to tears. Then a friend of mine found out I was looking for work and offered me a temporary position at their stand in Green Castle Farmers' Market making $100 a weekend. Jonas also worked a little for his dad, and between the two of us we were making around $1,000 per month. In our "spare" time we worked on Jake's mobile home (in which we lived)—Jonas did the plumbing and some electrical stuff while I worked on things like cleaning and painting. Life was busier than ever, but we all felt happy to be around family again.

Then came another blessing out of the blue, another fateful moment putting me even more firmly on the path to starting Auntie Anne's Soft Pretzels.

❖

Late one Thursday night, Jonas and I sat in the small mobile home we were fixing up for my brother Jake, when one of his kids knocked at the door.

"You've got a call, Auntie Anne," one of my nieces told me.

We didn't have a phone line to the trailer, so if someone wanted to reach us, they would call Jake's house and then we would go in and take the call.

I walked the short distance to Jake's house and picked up the phone.

"Hello?"

"Hi. I know you don't know who I am, but I heard you're back in town and looking for work. I started a market down in Burtonsville, Maryland, and need some help on Fridays and Saturdays. Are you interested?"

"Sure," I said, a little disappointed that it wasn't a waitressing job. "I have nothing better to do. When do you need me to start?"

"How about tomorrow morning?"

"Sure."

That was that. I worked for him that weekend at the Burtonsville Farmers' Market, and it went great. The job was all about customer service and cleaning, which suited me perfectly. But there was one other important point—our main product was soft pretzels.

Anyway, I worked hard that weekend and enjoyed myself. But there were still a few restaurants I was waiting to hear back from regarding being a waitress. I would have been more comfortable waiting on tables, and I thought I could probably make better money through tips. Plus, the five-hour round-trip drive to Burtonsville seemed like a waste of time.

On Tuesday the stand owner paid me another unexpected visit.

"Anne, you did a great job this weekend."

"Thanks, I really enjoyed myself."

"Good. Good. Anne, I'd like you to manage the stand for me."

Silence.

Me, a manager? I nearly laughed in his face. I had no managerial experience, no idea what to even do with the money at the end of the day. Payroll? Employees? Inventory? I had never done any of it. Yet somewhere deep inside of me, I felt intrigued by the challenge and knew I could do it.

"Well, I don't know. I've never done that type of thing before. I don't have any experience."

"That's okay, Anne. You're a hard worker. I saw you flying around that place on Saturday. I can teach you everything you need to know. I really think you're the right person for the job. I know you can do this."

After talking a little longer with him, my mind was made up.

"Okay. If you think I can manage your store, then I'll give it a try."

❖

The next day I got two calls back from restaurant owners who said they would hire me. I turned them down simply because I didn't want to let my new employer down—secretly, I desperately wanted to accept their offers, and if they would have called a day earlier, well, who knows how things would have turned out. In any case, I began my short stint as manager—little did I know that only a few short months stood between me and owning my very first business.

CHAPTER FOUR

The $6,000 Loan

Being in your own business is working eighty hours a week so that
you can avoid working forty hours a week for someone else.

—RAMONA E. F. ARNETT

I sat in one of the front pews in our old church, the same church I worried so much about returning to. A deep red carpet lined the floor, and the open ceiling peaked high over our heads. A ten-foot dark wood cross hung solidly on the wall behind the pastor, witnessing his every move. On that particular day I can't remember who gave the sermon. Absorbed by what he said, I leaned forward, all of my attention focused on the platform.

Suddenly, in the middle of the sermon, I felt a gentle tapping on my shoulder. I looked around and saw a stranger. The person didn't say a word, only beckoned to me with her index finger to follow her out of the main auditorium, and even though I didn't know who she was, for some reason I trusted her. I stood up, feeling slightly embarrassed about getting up in the middle of the service, but no one else in the congregation of more than three hundred even acted as though they saw me moving—it was as if I didn't exist.

I followed out the back doors and into the foyer, then around a side hallway and down a long corridor with rooms on each side. I recognized the hallway—it led to all of the Sunday school classrooms in the church. The tile floor felt cool under my feet, and the walls were cement blocks painted white. One of the doors on the right led into the nursery, the same nursery where twelve years ago Angie played with her little friends and cousins. The person I followed turned into the nursery. As I followed her into the small room, I heard a child laughing.

Standing there in front of me, could it be?

"Oh, Angie," I said, running over to her and getting down on my knees, looking into her deep blue eyes.

"Hi, Mommy," she said as plain as day.

"Oh, Angie," I said again, unable to say anything else.

"They are taking good care of me, Mommy," she said in her pixie voice, and then I knew the others in the room, as well as the one I followed, were angels. I bent forward and felt Angie's diaper, one of those "old-fashioned" cloth ones, nothing like the ones my daughters use on their children. On the day of the accident, I let Angie leave the house in a wet diaper, and it had always bothered me so much that she had died that way.

Angie laughed.

"Don't worry, Mommy," she said again, smiling, as I checked her diaper.

Her diaper felt soft and dry. What a relief!

"They are taking good care of me, Mommy. Don't worry. When Aunt Fi drove over me, two big beautiful angels carried me into heaven. Now I'm picking flowers, playing with all the other children, and I even get to sit in Jesus' lap."

Then came that strange feeling of emerging into reality. The room and Angie and the angels all started to fade and swirl. I fought to stay there, to stay in that dream, but the reality of that cold autumn morning somehow gripped me and pulled me into real life. Through blurry eyes I looked at the clock: 4:30 a.m. Time to get up, time to get ready for market.

❖

I took a quick shower, the water and the heat helping me wake up, before walking out into the kitchen and grabbing a mug of coffee. Our living quarters were small and cramped and left quite a bit to be desired, but I had purpose. I was a manager. The morning still slept in darkness, but I hummed while closing the heavy door behind me and walked out to the narrow sidewalk—I spotted my van and smiled. I was so proud of that van.

My boss had told me that part of my job as manager would be to pick up the Amish girls who worked for us, which is why I had to leave so early. He told me I should buy a new van to taxi everyone around in, so I went on down to the local Dodge dealer to look around. There was a particular kind of van popular back then, and I had always wanted one, but when I looked at the sticker price, my heart sank. I knew my and Jonas's credit fell well short of the requirement. But I needed that van. I talked to my boss about it, and he said to go ahead and buy it—he would even co-sign on the loan for us! And the money he paid me for mileage covered the monthly van payment! Every morning I climbed into that van so thankful to God, and my boss, for the blessing.

By the time I picked up the last Amish girl and headed for

the farmers' market in Burtonsville, Maryland, light began creeping up over the eastern edge of the world. A feeling of warmth and happiness filled me, a satisfying feeling that only comes when you are making something of yourself, forging ahead in the world with hard work and willpower. On those early mornings, I felt that I could do anything.

We arrived at market, and everyone piled out, yawning and waking up but usually laughing too—we were a fun group, we worked hard together, and we knew that smiling and laughing made the long days go faster. We walked down the aisles crowded by produce and baskets and barrels overflowing with things for sale. The stands were brand new but simple, nothing fancy. Some of the food stands looked more permanent, with walls and high ceilings. The main hall was large; in the mornings you could hear it start to wake up as people called out to one another. The market's grand opening lay only a few months behind us, and an air of fresh excitement radiated throughout the building.

In our stand we cleaned and prepared for the day, turning on ovens and stocking up inventory. We sold soft pretzels, home-made potato chips, and mountain pies, pastries filled with beef and vegetables, while also selling candy in an adjoining stand. Usually we got ready with time to spare, and I headed down to where one of the tenants served an inexpensive but hearty breakfast over a tall counter. We sat on the round stools and chatted about the goings-on in the market—who was getting married, who was having children, who was selling their stand or hiring more help. In some ways that market group seemed extremely diverse, but there were more similarities than differences: most of us who worked there grew up in Lancaster County, most of us were Amish or grew up in the

Amish-Mennonite community, none of us was scared of hard work, and we were all trying to get ahead. I felt responsible for my family, trying to bring in some extra money so that Jonas could push ahead with his dream of providing free counseling to those who needed it. Already he counseled two days a week and studied two more days, and I felt proud that by working I could allow him to continue. Yet that feeling of responsibility brought back a lot of memories from my childhood.

A Thursday afternoon in 1961. I was twelve years old at the time and had only recently heard the whispers, the crying, the hushed discussions about how relatives would help us in our time of financial difficulty. I entered the house that afternoon, like every Thursday afternoon in those days, knowing Mom would be at market with Dad. We had suffered some serious financial setbacks in the previous years, so Mom would go along to market to try to save on labor costs while the eight of us kids stayed home and looked after things. My allergies forced me inside while the rest of my brothers and sisters worked in the garden or the barn, and I looked around for the note I knew waited for me, a note from Mom addressed to "Annabetz" listing the number of pies and cakes needed for that weekend's trip to market.

"10 cherry pies, 10 apple pies, 10 shoefly pies . . ." The list went on. Occasionally the heaviness, the responsibility, the wish to run outside on such a beautiful summer day, the sadness that Mom wasn't home—all of these things would combine and bring tears to my eyes. Yet arriving in the basement meant a time for action, and action has always formed a welcome distraction. Soon I was making pie crusts, pie filling, and icing for the cakes, all the while humming to myself, wishing my sisters could be there singing with me. In what seemed the blink of an eye, the work vanished, fifty or sixty pies and cakes baked slowly in the huge stone oven, and I thought to myself with a smile how Daddy would yell out to the customers in the market that they had the best cakes and pies around.

"Get your fresh, hot, soft pretzels here!" I would yell out to the morning, thinking about Daddy and how he would bring in the customers with his loud voice booming through the market. But this was Burtonsville in the fall of 1987, and I was managing another stand, not working at Daddy's. I often thought of Daddy, how proud he would be to see me in there managing and working hard. I find that a lot of times I'm still working hard for him, even though he's not around anymore.

Just before 9:00 a.m. we started work in earnest, filling up the pretzel display and waiting on the first customers to arrive. From that point on the day blurred in one long hustle and bustle and whirlwind of work: roll pretzels, help customers, clean, roll more pretzels, help more customers, make sure all the employees get their breaks, prepare for the lunch and dinner rush. Finally the day eased off to a slow finish as the market emptied. Clean the equipment. Wash the dishes. Pile into the van. Drive home.

I got home late Friday night dog tired but happy. Sales were good, not as good as we needed them to be, but every week showed steady improvement. I stayed up for a little while talking with Jonas about the day but went to bed at a decent hour—the next morning it all started again.

Saturdays were even better than Fridays because my daughters went to market with me. Both of them worked hard, and LaVale, even though she had only just turned eleven, pretty much ran the candy side of the stand by herself. I found myself completely surprised at how well she dealt with customers and handled the money. At the end of the day, she even gave me a complete inventory with a list of her recommendations as to how much I should buy for the following week. She always knew exactly what I wanted her to do just before I told her—I often called her my little soul mate. I felt so close to her in those days.

Of course there were trying times even then, like the time I found LaVale and her cousin smoking a cigarette behind my brother's house. Or the time LaVale and that same cousin took her older sister's car for a joyride. But even those things seemed rather innocent at the time—sure, they gave me some stress and worry, but worse things could happen, right? LaVale and I still remained close, even through those relatively small conflicts. Unfortunately, things would get much worse in our relationship over the coming years.

My relationship with LaWonna was another story. Things changed when we first arrived in Pennsylvania, and I worried about her constantly. One of the major changes was her getting a driver's license. I could feel her pulling away from me and felt disappointed at the choices she made. I also thought she was getting into trouble, but little did I know just how serious her trouble was becoming, or how much her past haunted her. Anyway, some of that frustration, on both of our sides, spilled over into our time working together at the market stand, until one day she approached me.

"I just can't work for you anymore, Mom. I like you as a mom, but I just can't work for you!"

I felt devastated. The fact that LaWonna didn't want to work with me hurt me deeply. We found her another job at a local pharmacy, but despite eliminating the stress that came from working together, our relationship continued to deteriorate. I took her decision not to work with me as a very personal rejection, something that made me feel inadequate as a mother and also as the friend I thought I should be to her. Couple my crumbling relationship with LaWonna with lingering guilt regarding my past, and depression began creeping in.

❖

As always, I hid my feelings well by staying busy and rushing about from here to there, an easy thing to do since being the manager of a small business required it: market on Friday and Saturday, church on Sunday, banking on Monday, running errands on Tuesday and Wednesday, looking over the inventory and picking up ingredients on Thursday, and then back to market again on Friday. And I loved every minute of it. I made $200 per week plus mileage. That meant I was making $800 to $1000 a month plus the use of the van basically for free, and Jonas was able to counsel more people, spend more time studying. We were really doing it, we were living out our dream, and apart from my low self-esteem, I enjoyed life and work and never considered doing anything else.

We could both feel the momentum gaining: week after week more people came to him about their troubles, their broken marriages, their difficult children, their past abuse or current addictions. Soon he met with eight to ten people each week, and I joined him in the sessions if I could. But running the market stand began taking over my life.

I completely immersed myself in the business, adjusting the menu and eventually emphasizing the soft pretzels as much as possible because of their low cost and increasing popularity. I eventually persuaded my boss to go to just soft pretzels on the one side of the stand, while still selling candy on the other side. I also took care of the books, tracking payments and sales and deposits. When Christmas came around, there was a Christmas party to attend, something I never even thought about, and I received a generous Christmas bonus! Financially we still lived month to month, but things felt secure.

Then another turning point: early in the new year a friend of mine told me there was a market stand for sale at the Downingtown Farmers' Market. They sold pizza, stromboli, and (the reason she called me) soft pretzels. I never planned on buying my own business—far from it—and felt fortunate just to be managing the stand I already worked at, but Downingtown was only a thirty-minute drive from our house, and the long journeys to Burtonsville every week were starting to wear on me. My friend gave me the details of the people who owned the store and even found out by asking around that they had been trying to sell for quite some time. My initial thought was that they would want way too much money, yet they seemed to want out, and I began to wonder if I should look into it.

But I also felt very committed to my boss. I couldn't leave him without a manager. The whole idea of abandoning him and his business nearly kept me from even calling the stand owners, but in the end I thought, *It can't hurt to just call, and besides, a lot of market stands sell for $100,000 or even more—most likely it will probably be well out of our price range.* I wrote their names down and decided to give them a call when I had a chance.

❖

"Hi, my name is Anne Beiler. Are you the ones selling the stand in the Downingtown Farmers' Market?"

"Yes, we are."

"I'm interested in buying your stand. How much are you asking for it?"

A moment of quiet deliberation on the other end of the line. I nearly said, "Okay, thank you," before they even spoke, so sure was I that the price would be unthinkable for Jonas and me.

"$6,000," said the voice on the other end of the line.

After asking a few more questions, I hung up the phone and just stared into space for a few moments. $6,000. That was hardly anything at all compared to what I expected the price to be. The sum just kept running through my mind. $6,000 . . . $6,000 . . . $6,000 . . . Jonas stood there with me in the kitchen and I turned toward him.

"They want $6,000. That's all they want for the stand."

Jonas waited there beside me while I thought some more. Even though the price came in much lower than I expected, $6,000 was still $6,000. It might as well have been $100,000, since we didn't have either amount saved up. Still, an incredibly strong feeling began welling up inside of me, the feeling that I should buy the stand, and I blurted out my feelings to Jonas.

"I just think I need to call them back and tell them I want it. I mean, $6,000. I thought it would be at least $100,000."

Jonas didn't even hesitate.

"Well, honey, if you feel like you should do it, just do it. Pop will give you the money." By Pop he meant his dad.

"Do you think he would?"

"Well, you know he's been telling us if we want to buy a house he would loan us the money. If he has the money to do that, why wouldn't he loan you just $6,000?"

I turned back to the phone, almost shaking. I called the stand owners back, only a few minutes after we first spoke.

"Hello?"

"Hi, this is Anne Beiler calling back. I would like to buy your market stand for $6,000." Even then I thought perhaps I heard the price wrong during the first call, or maybe they sold the stand in those precious few minutes while Jonas and I spoke.

We agreed on the price, and I told her I would drop a check off at her house the following week. I still hadn't seen the market stand or even secured the money to buy it! But I felt as though I was doing the right thing. Immediately after the phone call, Jonas and I hopped in our car and drove over to Jonas's parents' house.

We told Pop the story, and then Jonas asked him for the money.

"Well, sure I'll give you the money," he said without even a moment's hesitation.

He wrote out the check at the kitchen table and handed it to me. It felt heavy in my hands, simply because of the amount. No one had ever handed money to me like that. The feeling of physically taking that check from him laid such a feeling of gratefulness and responsibility over me that I hardly knew what to say.

"Pop," I said, my voice shaking. "I don't know when I'll ever be able to pay this back, but I promise you, I will."

He just looked at me with a loving, steady gaze and said three words.

"I trust you."

Jonas and I walked back to the car. I was stunned, could feel the check bulging in my pocket like a heavy rock. By the way I acted, you might have thought I had just been given $1 million. The following week I dropped the check off while Jonas traveled to Downingtown to check out the market stand we'd bought. In only a few short days I went from managing someone else's stand to purchasing my own. The only thing left to do was tell my boss about my plans.

My heart raced. It was a Monday, and I sat across the table from him at a local restaurant and ordered my breakfast. He probably thought we were having one of our usual meetings to discuss the business, the staff, and how things were going at the market stand in Burtonsville. He had no idea I was about to give him my resignation. He also had no idea I couldn't even work for him that very weekend, only five days away.

But I planned everything to the tee. My sister Becky would take over as manager until he could find someone, and I even hired a few extra workers just to make sure he wouldn't be short of help. I would give the van to Becky for her to use, and she would provide transport for the Amish girls who needed rides. Finally I blurted it out, told him I bought a market stand and needed to be there that weekend. I told him all the plans I'd put in place to ease the transition and apologized again and again for the short notice.

Once again, he proved to be a man full of understanding. He appreciated that I arranged for everything, even though I had to leave on such short notice. I couldn't be more thankful to him for the opportunity he gave me at Burtonsville, and I still feel so thankful to him for believing in me—his confidence that I could make his little market stand work instilled in me such drive and self-belief that I can't picture my life today without his positive influence. But he still had an important role to play over the coming months as I transitioned into my new store.

I sat quietly at the kitchen table. The cold winter air tried to push its way in through the door or the cracks around the window, but we sat snug in our little burrow. A small lightbulb lit up the room; behind me stood two closed doors, one led to my and Jonas's bedroom, where Jonas slept quietly, and the other to LaWonna and LaVale's bedroom. LaVale lay quietly in her bed, but I could tell by the creaking that she was still awake. The early hours of the morning came, and still LaWonna didn't return.

I wanted to go look for her but, without the first idea of where to begin searching, decided to just wait. A few weeks earlier LaWonna had stayed out late, and Jonas went looking, driving the endless back roads and scouting a few of her friends' houses, to no avail. While he drove those country lanes, he experienced a revelation—he would never find her driving around like that, and by chasing her into the wee hours of the morning, he allowed her decisions to shape his life, deprive him of sleep, and cause him to worry. *No more*, he thought to himself as he turned the car toward home. *No more*. And somehow he wiped his hands clean of the situation, still confronting her when necessary, still helping me raise the girls, but managing to separate himself from the things over which he had no control. I, on the other hand, was not nearly that strong.

I wept. I prayed. I read my Bible. Still she didn't come back. These nights happened time and time again, and still I would wait up for her. At first when she came back, she would completely ignore me, and I would give her the silent treatment in return as she went into her room and slammed the door behind her. At other times we would have discussions that left both of us feeling angry and wronged.

One night I followed her into her room.

"Honey, what's wrong?" I asked.

Her eyes looked very sad.

"I don't know what's wrong, Mom. I just don't think I can live here anymore."

❖

Should you decide to look for the first Auntie Anne's Soft Pretzel stand, you would need to go down Route 30 in eastern Pennsylvania just west of Philadelphia and take the Downingtown exit. After driving through a small town that reminds you of just about every other small town in America, you would need to go through a few intersections. Then you would need to go back in time to the late 1990s, to the years before they bulldozed the market and turned it into one of these large box-store strip malls.

Don't get me wrong: When we first visited our new stand, the one we'd just bought for $6,000, the last words to spring to mind would have been "life" or "energy." The market was old and tired, the tenants dissatisfied, and the customers disenchanted. My previous market stand had always felt alive and exciting. The first day I worked there had been the market's first day of business, and everyone could feel the energy. Customers loved what we offered, stand owners were motivated by the potential to turn the market into something successful, and all of this transferred to more lively employees. Downingtown, on the other hand, was old and in decline.

Jonas and I still felt optimistic about our stand, but the atmosphere of the place dampened our enthusiasm. All of the stand owners seemed to have so much to complain about: there weren't enough customers, the rent was too high, the parking lot was too dirty. The employees just kind of sat there and stared at you. As we walked down to our end of the market, things seemed a bit more lively. It was a newer section with mostly Amish stand holders. But I must admit worry began creeping into my mind when I compared the chemistry of that market with the one I'd worked at just the weekend before.

During the first weekend, the previous owners of our stand helped us learn the operational ropes, taught us how they did things, and gave us their recipes—all of the normal handover stuff. They were eager to leave, and I couldn't wait to get started.

The first thing we did that week was clean and renovate the store to make it more functional. The stand was one of the larger locations in the market—we had seating and sold pizza, strombolis, soft pretzels, and ice cream. We cleaned the equipment, and Jonas added some touches of his own to make the operations flow more smoothly. My youngest brother, Carl, even showed up one day to help us with the changes. When I tried to pay him for his work, he just shrugged it off.

"We're just glad you guys are back," he said. "This is what family is for." He couldn't possibly have known how touched I was—after all we went through during our years in Texas, after feeling so nervous that my own family wouldn't accept me because of all the mistakes I'd made, here they were helping me out so much. With their help we finally got the store just right: everything was sparkling clean, the equipment was ready to go, and we were fully stocked for our first week of sales. I could hardly sleep at night.

❖

When I did sleep, my nights filled up with strange dreams and premonitions. Whether stressed about making the business work or lying in bed waiting for LaWonna to come home, I found my nights becoming more and more restless. I remember one dream in particular.

Cruising down the road in our old '73 Cadillac, the blue one we moved to Texas in, suddenly I saw Angie in the car with me. I couldn't believe it, and I remember feeling very excited to see her. She looked just like LaWonna, only taller and with long dark hair, and she was probably around fourteen years old. Absolutely beautiful. I don't remember how she got there in the car with me, but immediately I said, "Oh, Angie, let's go see Aunt Vern!" Vern is my brother Merrill's wife, and she became a close friend to me during those first years back from Texas.

I went in the front door of Vern's house and walked up the steps. I stood at the top and yelled down the hallway, "Vern, someone is here to see you."

She came out of her bedroom, and Angie was standing beside me.

"And who is this?" Vern asked, smiling.

I said, "Vern, you don't know who this is?" I couldn't believe she didn't recognize her immediately.

Suddenly Vern's face nearly exploded with excitement and joy. "Oh my, this is Angie! You look just like LaWonna! Anne, you must be so happy!"

They hugged and cried and laughed, and I remember feeling so grateful that Vern could see her too.

The three of us left the house and got in the car.

Vern sat in the front seat with me and said, "Let's go see Aunt Beck. She would love to see Angie." So we headed off down those wonderful country lanes, driving between fields of high corn, a blue sky above us. With Angie and Vern with me in the car, the three of us off to show Angie to my sister Becky, I couldn't have felt happier or more carefree.

Vern and I sat in the front seat talking, and when I looked in the rearview mirror, Angie had turned into a little three-year-old girl. I kept looking back then quickly talking to Vern, trying to distract her so she wouldn't see what was happening—for some reason I was embarrassed by Angie, afraid Vern would see her acting like a baby and slobbering all over everything.

Finally we arrived at my sister Becky's house and we went up to the kitchen. When we walked in, she looked over at us and said hello.

Excitement choked my voice as I said, "Becky, I brought someone to see you."

"Should I know who this is?" she asked.

What was wrong with everyone? Why didn't they see what was going on? Why didn't they recognize Angie?

"Don't you know who this is?" I asked Becky, my voice

changing to a whine. By now Angie had returned to her fourteen-year-old body.

"You are Angie!" Becky exclaimed, her eyes glowing. "You look just like LaWonna!"

Suddenly I woke up.

Immediately upon waking, I felt a realization stir up from deep inside of me. Perhaps it was a mother's intuition, or perhaps God told me. Whatever the case, the strangest feeling overwhelmed me, a feeling that something had happened to LaWonna when she was only three or four years old. I knew that LaWonna was that little girl in my dream whom I felt embarrassed about. But what could have happened to her? From that point on I never stopped wondering, but nothing I imagined came close to the reality of the past she was hiding.

A few weeks or months later, my fears were confirmed when I went to pray with a friend of mine. LaWonna dated her son, and we would meet from time to time to pray for our children, asking God to keep them safe.

During this particular prayer time, my friend and I talked for a while before I left. I could tell something bothered her, so I asked her about it. She said that during the week she came home earlier than expected and heard her son and LaWonna upstairs—LaWonna sounded very upset.

My friend didn't know what to do. Should she go upstairs? Were they fighting? She waited until LaWonna left, then asked her son what all the noise had been about. He told her that LaWonna had told him a terrible secret, something he couldn't tell anyone else.

"Something horrible happened to her when she was a little girl, Mom," he said. "But we can't tell anyone about it."

I remember that first day in my market stand, the relief that only comes with the serving of a first customer, the elation you feel when the register begins filling with money and you know you can at least pay the rent, pay the employees, and have enough left over to buy the ingredients for next week. We flew around that stand like greased lightning, yelling playfully back and forth to each other, making customers smile, serving only the best. But what I'll remember most is how nervous I felt, how happy to be doing something on my own, and how love overwhelmed me when a deliveryman walked up the aisle, stopped in front of my stand, and dropped off a bouquet of flowers with a note:

You can do this, honey.

Love, Jonas

At the end of those first few weeks, I felt two things very strongly, the first being that we could definitely make this thing work. Sales went up each week, customers seemed happier than ever, and people loved the life and energy my family and I brought to the stand. By now both of my sisters, my daughters, a few in-laws, and even nieces and nephews worked for me at the stand, and we had tremendous fun working together. The market was only a thirty-minute drive from my house, so even though I was busier with work, I wasn't away from home any more than when I ran Burtonsville. I felt positive about the new venture and knew we would make a success of it.

The second main thought in my mind at the end of those first few weeks almost makes me laugh when I think about it, considering the fact that I ended up building the largest soft pretzel chain in the United States: the pretzels we made during those first few weeks tasted horrible, and I couldn't wait to stop selling them.

CHAPTER FIVE

From a Store to a Business

The secret of business is knowing something nobody else knows.

—ARISTOTLE ONASSIS

I often wonder if anyone could hear the six of us singing on those short winter afternoons when I was a little girl. Perhaps someone driving through central Pennsylvania stopped on one of the old country roads to get their bearings, or perhaps one of our neighbors walking from field to hard brown field paused, listened, and heard our voices carried by the wind, singing. Often Daddy would ask us to sing or Mom would take the lead and start a song. Singing and working seemed a natural combination: working hard was as necessary as breathing, and when I sang I felt myself rising up and out of those hard times, floating on a cloud of happiness.

I'm thinking of sometime around 1958 when we lived on the farm, in the dark hours of winter when the afternoons were cut short and the fields looked as though they would never support life again. Daddy would round up those of us old enough to work and, along with Mom, lead us out to the tobacco barn. Tobacco was Daddy's winter crop, and we knew how important it was to box the leaves and get them ready to sell.

The wind whipped around that old barn, howling through the cracks, and our fingers grew numb as we worked. Quickly we fell into a rhythm: Daddy, Jake, and Sam (my two older brothers) stripped the tobacco from the stalk while Becky, Mom, and I gingerly placed the dried leaves in sizer boxes, a long leaf in a long box, a short leaf in a short box. Working together we could keep store-bought food on the table until the spring came with its garden vegetables to eat and sell.

Soon the light coming through the cracks in the barn walls became barely enough to see by, and Mom would rise without a word and go inside to prepare supper. Then Daddy would take my place and send me inside to help. I ran out the barn door and gasped as the cold dashed through my thin work dress (the only one I owned)—behind me I heard Daddy's voice admonishing the boys to move faster now; they had to keep up with the tobacco stripping on their own while Daddy boxed the long leaves.

Arriving inside, I felt as though I had died and gone to heaven—the warmth, the smell of good food cooking, the chatter and commotion of my four younger siblings: Fi, Dale, Merrill, and Carl. They were playing, learning to crawl or walk. I stood by the stove and warmed my hands, feeling the tingle rising through my arms, flushing my cheeks and nose. Then I helped Mom get the food together and fill the clear plastic cups with fresh water. We depended entirely on each other in those days.

Mom would check on the same three things every time: bread, water, and chairs. Did everyone have bread, did everyone have a glass of water, and were there enough chairs around the table? There were ten of us, and sometimes finding all of the chairs took a little time.

Finally I wrapped my sweater around my shoulders and dashed back out to the barn. When I returned inside, Daddy and the older ones came right behind me.

Fast-forward twenty-nine years to a Saturday in February 1988. Enter a busy farmers' market in Downingtown, Pennsylvania, a rather run-down sort of place that seemed tired and fading. Yet there I was, proud store owner for nearly a month, and I couldn't have been happier. Working hard and making a few minor changes meant the store was busier than ever, and I couldn't believe my good fortune. But something that made me even happier: the fact that my whole family could again work together.

The girls joined me on the weekends: LaVale, now eleven going on twenty-one, was our little pizza maker. With Aunt Fi helping, she made the dough, formed the pizza, added the toppings, and baked them to perfection, loving every minute of it. LaWonna even came back into the fold, so to speak, leaving her job at the pharmacy to work with us at the market stand. Her main task was making the strombolis and helping customers. I found myself continually amazed at both her and LaVale's ability to handle even the toughest of customers. But I also know I demanded perfection, perhaps too much at times. Still, we worked together in rhythm, busier every weekend, as a family. The girls even started getting along better—instead of seeing that as a potential threat to LaVale's innocence, I chose to see their positive relationship as evidence that our family was growing closer. I can see now how unrealistically optimistic I was in those days, grasping at any sign of familial happiness, feeling as though perhaps my girls and I were coming back together, perhaps old wounds were mending. Perhaps, but in the end it proved a brief period of peace.

In the meantime Jonas tinkered with everything: he made the pretzel dough, put up new signs, fixed broken cabinet hinges, put up more signs, and on and on he continued, always fixing things. During the week he continued to work hard at counseling. I didn't know until recently how awkward it felt for the girls to have strangers constantly parading through our living room, but LaVale once referred to those ladies as "forever trapped in the 1980s with their bad perms, smelling of cigarette smoke." I never thought how strange it must have been for my daughters, eating a dinner they scraped together for themselves (while I ran a business) and hearing women they didn't know crying in their daddy's study. I think some of the discomfort came from LaWonna and LaVale's not knowing what to say or do—do you say hi and risk embarrassing those being counseled by even acknowledging their presence (and the fact they were searching for help), or do you do what the girls normally did and just stare at the television, the floor, or blankly into space? But no matter how odd the situation, LaWonna remembers thinking to herself, *If anyone can fix these people, Daddy can.*

While Jonas experienced success in helping others with their problems, the pretzels proved to be a riddle I could not answer. They were, quite simply, horrible. They always came out pale and crusty around the edges, and we tried everything we could think of to make them as good as the pretzels we made at Burtonsville: more flour, less flour, more water, less water, bake them longer, bake them hotter, and on and on it went. I didn't have a particular affinity to pretzels at that point, but I did enjoy making them. Rolling the dough provided me with a therapeutic busyness, and I liked giving the customers a show to watch. But finally, after about a month of tinkering, I decided to focus on the pizzas and strombolis that sold so well. Besides, all of this tinkering with pretzel dough cost me a fortune in inventory, and I felt sick from all the money we wasted trying to get them just right. Jonas and I even sat down one evening and prayed together about it, asking God for wisdom regarding how to make the pretzels! He didn't seem to pay us much attention, though, as our attempts got worse and worse. But I wasn't giving God enough time.

Finally, on one particular Friday morning, I grumbled to Jonas.

"You know what," I announced suddenly, "I am just going to quit making these pretzels and we are going to focus on strombolis and pizzas. I've decided to take them off the menu board today."

"Well," Jonas said mysteriously, "before you give up on the pretzels, let me try something that might work."

I laughed.

"Hey, if you've got this great idea, just go ahead and give it a try!"

He listed a few different ingredients he wanted to add.

"What makes you think that would work?" I asked.

"I used to do some baking of my own when I was a kid," he said with a twinkle in his eye, "and my aunts taught me some things that I think might work with this recipe."

"If you think it's going to work, then go ahead and get the ingredients." I felt rather skeptical.

He took off his hat and apron and went to the local grocery.

When he returned, he brought an air of excitement along with the special ingredients. He put his apron back on and mixed the batch himself. He swept up everyone else with his enthusiasm, and soon our employees stood around the mixer waiting to see how the new recipe would turn out. Everyone, that is, but me. I just kept rolling the old dough, ready to take pretzels off the menu and be done with them.

In some ways Jonas's childhood resembled mine very closely: we both grew up in Lancaster County, Pennsylvania, in conservative communities (my family was Amish-Mennonite while Jonas's was Old Order Amish); we both learned the importance of hard work at an early age; and we both felt the importance of family and community in general. But even within a community such as ours, everyone experiences a vastly different life.

When Jonas reached the age of two, and his younger sister was only six weeks old, his mother went into hospital for gallbladder surgery. She arrived at the hospital a strong, healthy mother of four children, the type of person always on the move, always running from one project to the next. Months and numerous infections later, she arrived home, her motor skills completely deteriorated, near to death. Jonas had two unmarried aunts who moved in with the family, cooking the meals and raising the children. While his two older siblings worked the farm with his father, and his mother remained confined to her bed, Jonas was mostly told to stay inside and help his aunts with the cooking and cleaning. At first it would seem an insignificant event in Jonas's life, his learning to bake, but who are we to know when a seemingly minor event might prove to be otherwise? If not for Jonas's early exposure to cooking, Auntie Anne's Soft Pretzels never would have come into existence.

For years Jonas's house hovered under a cloud of sadness—on rainy days the children would have to play as quietly as possible while their mother lay in her bed. Would she ever get better? On a hot, dusty Sunday, Jonas, only three or four years old, walked to church, his little hand completely swallowed by the rough, calloused hand of his father. They went quietly down to where church was being held at Jonas's uncle's house. The dust rose, swirling around them as they walked. Jonas looked up at the bearded face, so high above him, and saw tears welling up in his father's eyes.

"Vas is letz?" Jonas asked his father in Pennsylvania Dutch. What is wrong?

His father looked down at him and sniffed his nose, hastily wiping the tears from where they sat around his eyes, pushing some of them deep into his long beard. Then he picked Jonas up and carried him awhile.

◆

We could all tell a difference even before we baked that dough—it smelled so good, and it rose in a way the other dough never did. We rolled a tray of six pretzels and put them in the oven. After only a minute in the oven, we were once again hit with the amazing smell!

"Jonas, those smell great," I kept saying. At that point I forgot about the old dough I had been rolling and felt just as eager as everyone else to taste one of these new pretzels. We stood around the oven, waiting.

Our lives in 1958 weren't all hard work and scraping to get by, boxing tobacco and making pies for market. No, our family always found ways to have fun. In fact, we would wait for weeks and weeks for a certain piece of news to arrive from a neighboring farm, and when it finally came there was a buzz around the farm all day. Chores were done quickly, in the hopes that the day would pass in the same way. We swallowed our dinner nearly whole. Daddy's silent prayers seemed to last an eternity. Evening chores never seemed to take so long. But after we finished everything, and after the sun had nearly set, we raced around putting on our warmest clothes, searching desperately for the skates we had put away the previous year, because, after all, the news had arrived that day: ice on the pond had frozen thick enough for skating!

Carrying our skates by their cold blades, we all raced to the pond. Usually we would arrive to find at least thirty or forty children laughing, tying skates, or warming themselves around the flickering bonfire. If snow had fallen recently, some of the boys busied themselves clearing the pond for ice hockey while others built snowmen or threw snowballs. Eventually a hockey game would start in the middle while the girls skated in circles around the game, holding hands, all smiles and laughter and light.

I would laugh and chatter with my sisters Becky and Fi and our friends from church, warming ourselves around the fire. At the end of the night when the hockey had ended, all of the children would hold hands, form a chain, and skate in circles around the ice, the innermost person acting as a pivot and sending the outermost person flying at breakneck speed as they "cracked the whip." I hung on to the end of the whip as the cold air burned against my teeth and made my eyes water; then they let me go and I shot off through the night, gliding on skates in a never-ending line, right up to the stars.

Eventually the time came to go home. The long walk on blistered feet with ankles sore from wearing skates for the first time that year didn't even seem a chore, so much fun the night had been. Plus, I knew that when we arrived home Mom would be waiting up for us with hot chocolate and mounds of buttered toast. When I finally managed to stumble to our bedroom, I would go down on my knees in a warm nightgown and say my prayers in front of the radiator, then snuggle into bed with thirteen-year-old Becky and seven-year-old Fi, arguing playfully about who got to sleep in the middle. Our room was so cold that sometimes when we woke up in the morning, the glasses of water we took to bed with us were frozen blocks of ice.

As we grew older, the parties changed. When I finally turned sixteen and was allowed to go out with my older sister, it felt like cracking the whip at a skating party, and I flew out into that new life with all the same speed and energy. One of the first people I met during this time was Sonny Beiler, a friend of Becky's. Stocky with curly jet-black hair and a love of life, he was nearly always playing pranks or making jokes or laughing, just for the sake of it. He embodied the way I saw my new life: full of fun and excitement.

One night I went with Sonny and Becky and another friend to a concert. Sonny seemed the center of attention, the life of the party. His eyes shone mischievously as the four of us spent the evening together. Then another one of those fateful encounters, when something happens that changes the course of your life: Sonny's younger brother appeared in the crowd, just for a moment. He smiled, came over. Sonny laughed and shook his hand, introduced him to me and my sister Becky.

"Becky. Anne. This is Jonas."

I can't say it was love at first sight. I was being swept up into a new life, a life of independence, and my first, brief introduction to my future husband came and went without much fanfare. That first meeting stood in line as only one of many exciting things that took place in those busy months, but it was a seed sown, a seed that was starting to grow, though still unseen.

Then came Sonny's birthday party, a surprise event arranged in Sonny and Jonas's body shop where they worked, beating old cars into shape. We went to so many of those parties: the frantic shushing, whispered yells of "He's here!" and "Quiet!" Then someone walks in—"Oh, it's not him!"—and the excited chatter rises again. Finally it *is* him: a hush falls over the room, the door opens, the light flashes on, and everyone hollers, "Surprise!"

During this party I saw Jonas for the second time, and this time he caught my attention. At sixteen, I had been on a few dates but nothing serious, and I felt nervous and giddy, wanting to talk to him but finding myself hanging back, waiting. Then came walk-a-mile.

Walk-a-mile was an Amish-Mennonite party game we played that allowed couples a semblance of privacy in a world where everything revolved around rules of propriety. The game went like this: a girl and a guy would decide they wanted to walk a mile, couple up, and do just that. During the walk we could get to know one another.

The suspense drove me crazy—I kept seeing Jonas across the room, kept wondering if he would ask me to walk a mile, and if he did, whether or not he would also ask me out on a date. The more I wondered, the more I found myself liking him. Finally, the moment came.

We walked and talked for a mile, and Jonas captured my heart with his boyish good looks, his charm, the way he and Sonny seemed so full of life when they were together. Plus, by that time Sonny and Jonas had left the Amish, which meant he dressed differently, stood out in the crowd. Old Order Amish dress is very plain, the men wearing hats and the women wearing head coverings. Their trousers and shoes and coats are black, and their shirts are solid colors. When Jonas was old enough, he decided he wasn't going to stay Amish, so he wore more contemporary clothing.

The longer the walk went on, the more desperately I wanted him to ask me on a date. But it didn't happen. Jonas was a shy boy, much less outgoing than Sonny, especially when Sonny wasn't around. Soon our walk-a-mile ended and we arrived, reluctantly, back at the party. I returned to my circle of friends.

I didn't have long to wait, though. Before I left that night, as I stood on the sidewalk outside the body shop, Jonas came outside and talked with me again. And he finally asked me out on a real date.

On the night of our first date, my nervous excitement couldn't be contained. I stood in the kitchen looking out the long lane, waiting, my stomach flipping and turning, my hands sweating. My three youngest brothers, Dale, eleven years old, Merrill, nine, and Carl, seven, stood in the kitchen with me, making me feel even more on edge. They wanted to meet this Jonas character; I just wanted him to arrive so that I could get on with the evening and stop feeling so jumpy.

Finally he arrived. I heard his '53 Ford with the loud muffler long before I actually saw it, but when I finally saw him turn the bend, I couldn't help smiling in giddy anticipation. The car arrived in three or four colors, in the middle of being rebuilt, and it charged up the lane, slowed beside the house, then turned around. When he shut off the engine, the silence it left behind stifled my breathing. Soon he came inside and I introduced him to the boys. Then we left, and the rest of that night is history. That marked the beginning of a long road, one full of much happiness and despair, one that would take us through some of the best, and most difficult, times of our lives.

But there is one other image I remember about that night: after Jonas dropped me off and drove away, I sat by my bedroom window and listened to his car. I could tell exactly which corners he turned and how many stops he made by the sound of his muffler, and if I counted the stop signs I could stay with him until the sound of the muffler faded, miles away.

Back in Downingtown in 1988, I stood around the ovens with the rest of our family and employees, waiting for those pretzels to come out. We all felt eager to try them, especially with that amazing smell starting to circulate around the stand. I looked at Jonas—he grinned and his eyes sparkled, but that didn't surprise me.

The pretzels came out, and those of us waiting tore into them like a bunch of vultures . . . and we couldn't contain our amazement! The difference in taste between those pretzels and the ones we had been making was completely indescribable. The new ones were soft and fluffy on the inside and crisp on the outside, tasted incredible, and melted in our mouths. I couldn't wait to sell them.

The first customer who bought a pretzel completely verified the success of Jonas's experiment. We all kind of watched as they bought their pretzel and walked away, reached into their bag, and took their first bite. They stopped. Turned around. Stared in amazement at the stand from which they'd just bought that small piece of heaven, then looked back at the pretzel as if they couldn't believe how good it tasted. And nearly every new customer we had from that day on did the exact same thing: taste, stop, turn, and shake their head in amazement.

By the end of that very first day, we were already selling more pretzels simply because the word had spread around the market. People were talking. "So and so told me I have to come down here and try one of your pretzels. They said it's better than cake!" I became more and more amazed at how the pretzel almost challenged people to compare it to something. "This is better than . . ." so many people would say, completing the sentence with some rather shocking examples! By the end of the day, business forced us to up our pretzel production, and I already wondered about the following week, how much inventory to buy and how many pretzels we would sell. Once again, Jonas had found a way to fix things.

During the next couple of weeks, business completely took off. In those days we sold pretzels for fifty-five cents each or three for $1.50, and soon we couldn't make the pretzels fast enough. We stopped selling pizza and stromboli just so we could keep up with pretzels, but to no avail. Soon it became normal to have a line of over thirty people stretching down the length of the hall and out the door that led to the other side of the market.

"Six pretzels for Mr. Brown," and I'd write the order on a receipt.

"Six pretzels for Mrs. Schmidt."

"Twelve pretzels for Mrs. Smith."

"Two dozen pretzels for Mr. West."

Order after order, and I rolled those pretzels as fast as I could. Jonas ran around tending ovens and making dough while the girls served customers, melted butter, counted change, and tried to keep everyone happy. We worked together like a well-oiled piece of machinery, but still we couldn't keep up with the demand.

I remember the end of one long day in particular, and it happened to be the first day we dropped everything else from the menu and sold only pretzels: we all felt exhausted, our feet ached, and the butter from the pretzels seemed to cake our skin in a greasy film. Cleaning was the last thing we felt like doing, but my store was always sparkling clean, so shortcuts were not tolerated. Finally, as the girls put the finishing touches on the store, I counted the money.

I started crying, and the girls came running.

"What's wrong, Mom?" they asked.

At first I couldn't answer, I felt so overwhelmed. I just cried and put my head in my hands. Finally I looked up at them, still crying for joy.

"Girls, we made $2,000 today."

Two thousand dollars in one day! I never dreamed of that kind of money. That night Jonas and I just laughed and laughed. We were giddy at how well that little market stand did for us, and for the first time we thought back to our friend's prophecy, wondering, *Is this what he was talking about? Where will things go from here?*

At some point between 1965, when Jonas and I started dating, and 1967, our friendship developed into a romance. We went on a date nearly every weekend, usually with another couple, many times with Jonas's brother Sonny and his girlfriend, Edna. Life seemed to pass quickly in those days, and Sonny often initiated the fun that we all had together.

He acted crazy, but in a way that brought out the happiness in all of us. The only thing he liked to do more than laugh was to make other people laugh, which would partially explain the time he and Jonas snuck into a house where some girls from church were having a party upstairs. They brought a friend with them, a possum that Sonny had just caught, and nudged it up the steps. They only had to wait a moment before shrieks and screams erupted, followed by every single girl in the house running outside. The possum ran out the door behind them, disappearing into the field. Jonas and Sonny ran to their car and laughed until their bellies ached.

Even my younger brothers were caught up in the atmosphere of fun that seemed to follow Sonny everywhere he went. In fact, my younger brother Merrill still remembers when he and Dale and Carl would watch in amazement as Sonny, sitting on the kitchen counter with his feet dangling below him, seemed to exert an incredible amount of force on his elbow and actually bend it backwards! Then he would do the same thing to his wrist, and to his hand, and to his fingers, until his entire arm appeared misshapen and his face glowed red with the effort. Awestruck, the three small boys went to bed, wondering how Sonny did it.

Shortly after Sonny and Edna were married in '67, the four of us and another couple went away to a cabin a few hundred miles away in the mountains. My parents let me go with Jonas because we went with a married couple, and I guess also because they trusted us. Sonny and Edna didn't stay for the entire weekend and went home one night before Jonas and I and the other couple returned.

The day after Sonny and Edna left, a loud knock sounded at the door. The four of us looked at each other in confusion—we didn't know anyone who lived in that area.

Jonas answered the door. Someone from town had come up with a phone message for a Jonas Beiler.

"I'm Jonas."

"I'm real sorry," the messenger said quietly. "Your brother Sonny is dead. He was killed in a motorcycle accident just this morning."

During the seven-hour drive back to Lancaster County, we didn't say a word to one another, only drove on in an unbelieving silence that something so horrible had actually happened. Occasionally Jonas would weep while he drove, then compose himself and continue on in silence. When Sonny died, almost with immediate effect, a silence fell over our relationship that would take me years and years to figure out and to come to terms with.

That year was the saddest time in my life up to that point, the first time I'd had to deal with the loss of such a close friend. At the time, I worked as a waitress at a truck stop, and during my entire shift I just couldn't wait to go home to lie in front of the family record player, put on Sonny's favorite album, and cry. I couldn't escape the realization that Sonny was gone and he wasn't coming back. These were no longer the tears I cried as a little girl walking into the basement, missing my mother. No, these were the tears of a young woman entering adulthood, and perhaps a little scared of what I was finding.

A growing unease between Jonas and me made everything even worse. Without Sonny we often found conversation hard to come by. Jonas turned inward, not knowing how to deal with the loss, not knowing what to do with his business at the body shop. Many nights I went on those dates with Jonas thinking, *Tonight I will break up with him. Lord, what should I do? Should I break up with him?* But night after night, week after week, we went out and came home, and still we hadn't broken up.

As the months following Sonny's death passed, I think both of us gradually began arriving at the same conclusion: we were meant to be together. I learned to love the new, quieter Jonas and adjusted to his times of inward reflection, but after my older sister, Becky, got engaged to her boyfriend, Aaron, I began to wonder if Jonas would ever pop the question or if we would just go on as we were, dating into eternity.

Then, after a trip to Florida with Becky's fiancé, Aaron, Jonas arrived back in Lancaster County with two things: a shattered elbow from falling off a sofa, and the resolve to ask me to be his wife. We were in the room beside the kitchen, the same room where years before I had cuddled up next to Beck and Fi after a long day's work, the same room where we always sang together as a family, the same room where I would often lie lamenting the loss of Sonny. Sitting on the sofa at our farmhouse, Jonas finally asked me the question I had been waiting so long to hear.

"Will you be my wife?"

"Are you serious?" I blurted out in astonishment.

It was January of 1968, and I said yes (after the initial outburst). Immediately we began talking through our future together, something we never discussed before. I guess it wasn't proper back then to talk about those kinds of things while you were just dating; but now we were engaged, so I fired off questions at an amazing rate: When should we get married? Where should we live? How many children should we have?

We decided to wait until September to marry so my older sister, Becky, could have her wedding first, and we also agreed to live close to Jonas's body shop, where he would continue fixing things. Finally, we both agreed that having four little girls would make the ideal family.

With two weddings being planned, that summer went quickly: first Becky's marriage to Aaron, and then September finally came. About two hundred and fifty chatting, overjoyed family members and friends attended, although everyone could feel the absence of Sonny. I wore the dress I had made: a stiff, metallic white material with silver metallic flowers, small buttons up the front, and knee length. A beautiful dress, and one I felt very proud to have made.

As we walked down the aisle and out the back of the church on that lovely autumn day, I couldn't believe it: I was Mrs. Jonas Beiler! Outside the church we kissed and cried, kissed and cried some more, kissing because of the joy we felt to finally be married, and crying because Sonny couldn't be there to experience the day with us.

From the reception held at the local fire hall, we drove back to my parents' house. In those days tradition dictated that the groom take the bride back to her house where they would go into her bedroom, she would change into her traveling clothes, and then they would leave on their honeymoon, being sent off by the whole family. As we walked into my room, the room I had shared with my sisters, we were suddenly standing alone in a bedroom for the first time, and I felt extremely vulnerable. I remember turning bashfully to Jonas.

"I may at least turn around while I change, mayn't I?" I asked.

I slipped out of my white wedding dress and hung it up on a hanger. My old life had ended, and I hung it up right there in that closet with my wedding dress. Behind me, in the form of a man named Jonas, sat my future. I couldn't have been happier.

We went downstairs and prepared to leave, but someone told me that Fi, fifteen years old at the time, sat weeping on the back porch. I was the second sister Fi said good-bye to in just a few months, and now she would have to sleep in her room all alone. It felt like too much for her to handle, so I sat with her for a while, just hugging her, not saying anything. Eventually, though, I had to leave; a new life was waiting for me.

I crawled into the car with Jonas, smiling, the family waving from the kitchen door. The engine roared to life and we drifted out the lane, dust rising behind us as we cruised off in Jonas's two-door hardtop 1960 Pontiac Bonneville, blue metal-flake paint, the nicest car in the neighborhood. Outside the car, the leaves were changing color, getting ready to fall. But inside the car, inside of me, a certain kind of winter melted, and I thought I could feel spring coming, just around the corner.

❖

Within only a week or two of the miraculous pretzel recipe transformation, people came from all around to try our soft pretzels. They are better than the best you've ever tasted, we eventually told people. No one disagreed. Little did we know at the time that we started the soft pretzel revolution—up until that point, no one tried to perfect the soft pretzel. They were sold by street vendors or as a part of an extended offering, but hardly ever as the main item of a larger shop.

The popularity of the pretzel changed our lives almost

immediately. Suddenly we found ourselves able to keep a couple of thousand dollars in savings, something we'd never done before. Money wasn't so tight, and we could afford some of life's little luxuries like eating out for dinner or paying rent for a real house and not just the corner of someone else's home. And I even started to enjoy the fact that everyone knew about my pretzels, at least in that small farmers' market—everyone knew I was the pretzel lady.

Being the pretzel lady became more than just a name, though. I found myself feeling more and more passionate about the product. I believed so strongly in the delicious pretzels we sold that I felt everyone must at least try them, and I did everything I could to get a pretzel to each person who passed my store. I started yelling out to people as they passed, asking if they'd ever tried my pretzels. I even gave away dozens of free pretzels every week—I just knew that if I could get people to try one, they would become regular customers.

No matter how quickly things changed over those few short months, one thing remained the same—Jonas and I remained as determined as ever to continue giving to people in need. Keeping that in mind, I constantly encouraged Jonas to continue his counseling services, even though many times he probably would have rather come with us to market where everything seemed exciting and new. To his credit, he persevered, continuing to meet with more and more people every week. But we also knew that giving financially played a huge part in our pretzel success, and at the end of each week I sat in front of that pile of cash and divided it into three piles—one in the amount we needed to pay the bills and buy inventory for the following week; another for the money we needed to pay our taxes; and last but definitely not least, money to give to our church that equaled 10 percent of what we made. I loved watching that pile of money grow taller and taller each week.

After one particularly busy day, I stood around with my sister Becky and our friend Emy. We couldn't stop talking about how many pretzels I sold and how people came from all over to try them. We knew the old sign reading "Pizza, Strombolis, Ice Cream, and Soft Pretzels" needed a replacement, especially since I no longer sold most of those items. The three of us brainstormed, trying to think up a new name for my pretzel shop.

We went through a number of generic names, such as "The Soft Pretzel Shop," but nothing stuck.

Finally Emy said, "Why don't you just call it Auntie Anne's Soft Pretzels? That's what everyone calls you anyway." *True*, I thought to myself. I had thirty-some nephews and nieces at the time, and when our extended families were together, it seemed that everyone called me Auntie Anne.

Jonas went home and made a cute little sign to hang outside the shop. It was white and cut in a decorative shape, and the letters were three dimensional in baby blue. The name and the colors would stay with us for the seventeen years I owned Auntie Anne's, but on that late spring day in 1988, we couldn't have imagined that in those next seventeen years we would build more than 850 locations bearing that name. In fact, if someone would have told us that, I am sure that Emy, Becky, and I would have laughed them out of town. But that just goes to show you that at no point in our lives can we have any idea about what waits around the next bend.

CHAPTER SIX

A Family Business

Coming together is a beginning; keeping together
is progress; working together is success.

—HENRY FORD

In June of 1988 our store at the Downingtown Farmers' Market had only been open for a mere four months, but we had already hit our stride. I enjoyed my newfound identity as "businesswoman extraordinaire," my relationship with my girls seemed headed in the right direction (oh, what an illusion that turned out to be!), and we literally couldn't make the pretzels fast enough. When it came to the bigger picture, everything seemed wonderful as well: Jonas and I were back in our hometown enjoying our families and old friends, we were better off financially than *we had been for a long time*, and Jonas's dream of providing people with counseling had become a reality. What more could we ask for?

But you see, there was one problem. One major problem. Most of my happiness depended on all of this stuff going well, especially the relationship I cultivated with my daughters. I looked back on the years in Texas I spent under that dark cloud, and I felt so guilty about the mother I had been (or hadn't been) to them. Now that things were smooth, I was happy. I felt that I filled the role of mother again. But happiness isn't joy, not even close, and I didn't realize that I walked right beside that old familiar abyss of depression.

How could I see the major arguments and disappointments with my daughters that lay just around the corner? How could I have known how big the business would grow, or how many new stresses that would add to my life? How could I have known that by 1995 I would be back at the bottom again, nearly as desperate as I was during the late seventies? The simple answer is I couldn't have known, and I walked along in innocent happiness, trusting too much in my own ability to hold it all together.

During these days of fragile happiness, Downingtown continued rolling along. My family, and especially my sisters, Fi and Becky, continued to support me as they always had. We took turns going in early to set up the shop, and we worked so hard together that everything felt like a game again, as if we went back in time twenty-five years to the height of our teenage frolicking. In the evenings, after a hard day's work, sometimes the three of us would sip coffee and sigh, lean back in our restaurant booth, and talk about how busy we were, amazed that we could sell so many pretzels. The next day we would start up again, enjoying each other's company and ready to work.

One day a young Amish girl from the barbecue chicken stand came down and started chatting with me. In those days my fame had spread far and wide (to that end of Downingtown Farmers' Market at least), and I guess she knew I owned the stand. Our new shop name, Auntie Anne's Soft Pretzels, caught on quickly, and soon everyone who knew I owned the stand started calling me Auntie Anne.

"Auntie Anne, there's a pretzel stand for sale at a farmers' market in Harrisburg," she said at some point in our conversation. "My parents go there. It's a good market. You should sell your pretzels there. It's called Broad Street Farmers' Market."

I just laughed.

"Oh, I don't know. I'm having fun here at Downingtown. Why would I want to open another store?"

"Well, you should just sell your pretzels up there," she kept insisting.

She came back two or three times, persistent in her belief that I should sell Auntie Anne's Soft Pretzels in Harrisburg, the capital city of Pennsylvania and about an hour's drive from where I lived. It amazed me then, and it amazes me now, that a little Amish girl would be so insistent that I go sell my pretzels at that market. Now, if a businessman approached me and reasoned with me, explaining that I made a good product and it would be a good business move and so on and so on, then perhaps I could understand. But this was not a businessperson with financial data, a five-year business plan, and numbers to back everything up. This was a teenage Amish girl, just a kid, and her persistence got a little annoying.

Finally I gave in.

"You know what, I guess I could go look," I said, perhaps more as a way of making her feel better than as an actual commitment to go and visit the market. Curiosity would eventually get the best of me, though, so after calling the market manager, Jonas and I decided to make a trip up there the following week.

We parked on the street in Harrisburg, not a very nice part of town back then. The market master met us and showed us inside. We were not impressed in the least by that inner-city farmers' market. The floors were dirty, the stands were old and run down, and the whole place smelled like the inside of a Dumpster. Even worse, not a soul seemed to be coming to the market. Market stand owners wandered the aisles alone, trying to find something to do.

On one side of the market sat the government buildings, office upon office upon office. On the other side of the market rose the projects, public housing, and I felt sorry for the people who had to live in those tall, drab buildings. Line after line after line of poor souls trapped in a place from which it must be so difficult to escape. At least that's how it made me feel when I drove through the neighborhood.

Jonas and I visited the Broad Street Farmers' Market on a Thursday, since Downingtown wasn't open on Thursdays, and even though this market was open, the place was dark and empty. We walked slowly behind the market master as he led us to the potential stand, and all the time I thought to myself what a waste of time our visit was turning out to be. Finally we sat down with the market master and he told us we could rent the location for $50 per week. Immediately in my mind something clicked. Fifty dollars a week? We paid $300 a week to rent the space at Downingtown. At that point in my life, as a new business owner in 1988, I could not have told you what the difference was between a profit and loss statement and a balance sheet, but I knew the difference between a rent of $50 and $300 per week: $13,000 per year, to be exact.

I will admit that at the time I felt bad that we took up the market master's day, and I almost felt obliged to take the location. But could we sell pretzels where there seemed so few people? Then again, there was the cheap rent to consider . . . Before I knew it, we signed the papers, and we owned another store.

I'll never forget that feeling driving home, the reality of the situation setting in, wondering with complete amazement, *What have I done?* I sat there quietly, watching the road fly by on a lazy summer afternoon, Jonas driving our little brown Toyota station wagon. The market master wanted us to open our store by July 4, only three weeks away. The stand would probably cost us around $5,000 to build and equip and prepare for our first week, nearly all of the money we'd managed to save at that point. Did we make the right decision?

"What's wrong?" Jonas asked.

"Honey, what is our problem?" I asked him. "Why are we doing this? Why aren't we satisfied with Downingtown? For the first time in life we're making money . . ." My voice trailed off before gathering steam again. "Besides, there's no one at the market! How do we know what's going to happen? Now we have to take all of our money out of savings, dump it into this place . . . I just don't know."

"We're not going to lose anything," Jonas said matter-of-factly. "$50 a week. All we have to do is sell one batch of pretzels each day and we'll be fine."

"Yes, I know, but we've got to build the store in three weeks! And it's taking up all our savings! It just seems so risky."

"You know what, though," he said calmly, "it's not a big risk. I'll build the stand for real cheap. We can use just about everything somewhere else if it doesn't work out."

Removed from the situation as I am today, I see many common threads in my life, one of which is Jonas's never-wavering encouragement. He always showed total confidence in me, whether it be in my skills as a businesswoman or as a mother or as a wife. Even after I disappointed that trust, he continued trusting me. He continued encouraging me. Without his confidence in me, especially during those years when I had such little confidence in myself, I never would have accomplished what I did. Or perhaps I should say *we* never would have accomplished what *we* did.

But in those days Jonas's belief in me wasn't quite enough. When we got back to the house, I got down on my knees by my bed and started asking God what he thought about it all.

"Lord, I don't understand this. Did I make a mistake?" I asked, feeling so overwhelmed and worried. I started crying, resting my head on the edge of the bed (I cried a lot in those days).

"Lord, I have to know, did we make a mistake here?"

Out of the blue a feeling washed over me, a feeling as tangible as when I received the flowers from Jonas on my first day alone at Downingtown, as tangible as when my family pitched in to help us get the Downingtown store ready. The feeling was one of peace and security, and I felt God saying one thing to me.

"Fear not, for I am blessing you."

This intervention completely interrupted my thought process, and suddenly I felt calm.

"Okay," I said, "I'll take it. I believe it," and I stood up and walked out of my room and told Jonas I felt ready to open Broad Street.

We went up there to Harrisburg, and in a few weeks we built that little store. My sister Becky managed Downingtown for me while I ran Broad Street, and suddenly things began to change. Auntie Anne's Soft Pretzels, after only five months in existence, was forced to grow—because of my natural, human inability to be in two places at the same time, I was forced to trust someone else to run my business at one of the two stores. Things would never be the same again, and the struggle within me to trust others in running my business became a common thread throughout the rest of my days as owner of Auntie Anne's.

On one hand, I completely trusted Becky. I knew she could manage Downingtown, and not just manage it but manage it well. On the other hand, I knew she did a few things differently than I did, and even though they were little things, it almost drove me crazy to think that I wasn't in control! Oh, if only I could have seen the future, when we would have hundreds of locations operating under different owners and managers and employees.

Meanwhile, the time came to open Broad Street. It didn't take long for my concerns regarding the potential for pretzels in that market to melt away—by the end of the very first day, we were competing with Downingtown in sales! We called back and forth, trying to outdo one another, and Broad Street nearly matched Downingtown dollar for dollar even with its shorter days (we were only open there from around 8:00 a.m. to 4:00 p.m.) and one-sixth the rent. Soon my weekend routine became fixed—I would close Broad Street in Harrisburg as quickly as possible, then take the hour-and-a-half drive to Downingtown and be there to finish out the day, see how sales went, and help close the store.

✦

Word of our success spread through the community much like yeast spreads through the dough, reaching every part. Jonas and I found our income more than doubling in no time at all. Both stores became busier and busier. At that time I believed our little business had finally reached its peak, and suddenly my friend's prophecy all the way back in Texas sprang to the forefront of my mind:

> "He will restore every broken relationship, he will give back to you more than you ever had before, he has a plan for you that you don't know about yet, but he will show it to you.
>
> "I just see so much for you guys. And it's not just spiritual blessing. It's, well, you think this house is beautiful? And don't get me wrong, it is. But I see God giving you things you wouldn't believe: I see houses, I see land, I see cars, I see, I just see all that stuff.
>
> "God is going to give it all to you. And you're going to start some sort of a business. I don't know exactly what kind, but that's the key. And it's going to happen within the first year of your arrival in Pennsylvania."

I couldn't believe it had actually come to pass. I couldn't believe things could change so quickly. And most of all, I felt horrible for laughing in my friend's face, in God's face, and for not trusting.

But suddenly something started happening that even our friend's prophecy didn't prepare me for, something none of us imagined: other people wanted to open their own Auntie Anne's Soft Pretzels stores.

❖

At first it happened with strangers tasting the pretzels for the first time.

"I'd love to sell these. Could I open a store?" they would ask as they inhaled a pretzel outside one of my two locations.

"Oh no," I would laugh. "There's only one Auntie Anne."

Soon more and more requests came in, serious business-people who would return week after week trying to get me to change my mind. While I felt a little jolt of excitement every time someone asked me if they could open a store of their own, my response stayed the same: "No, no, two locations are quite enough." But I guess two locations were not enough, and I felt myself beginning to give in when my family members started asking if they could open an Auntie Anne's.

Finally in the spring of 1989, a little more than a year after we sold our first pretzels at Downingtown, Jonas went to Saturday's Market in Middletown, Pennsylvania, with my brother Jake to talk to the owner of the market about open-ing an Auntie Anne's Soft Pretzels store. At that time Jake was a siding estimator for a local builder, but he wanted to own his own business and make some extra money. It wasn't long before we agreed a deal at Saturday's Market, and the first licensed Auntie Anne's was on the schedule to open. We called it licensing back then because we didn't understand that side of the business very well, but you'll see what a big part of our development the difference between franchising and licensing played in those early years.

Jake and Jonas built that store from scratch in just a couple of days out of two-by-fours and plywood. The countertops were butcher block Formica, and the front of the store consisted of handmade counters and generic Plexiglas. These days it can cost over $200,000 to start an Auntie Anne's location, but back then we didn't have leasing fees, attorney's fees, architects, brand-new equipment to purchase, or mall regulations to work around—we just built it how we wanted it to look and that was that. The store cost us a couple of thousand dollars to get up and running, and while we paid for the up-front cost, Jake paid us back $100 a week until it was all paid off, plus a 4 percent royalty. We still sold pretzels back then for around 50 cents a piece, but Jake only paid $24 a week in rent, so the costs were just right.

We were busy there right from the first Saturday, and once again the lines seemed to go on and on forever. We also started to notice that people found the whole process of rolling pretzels fascinating—even after they bought their pretzels and started eating them, they would often linger beside the stand for a long time, just watching us make the pretzels. Maybe we didn't notice this as much at our other locations because pretzels had been at those places before we arrived, but at Saturday's Market the novelty factor of hand-rolled pretzels became very apparent.

Then there was the lady from the market who came up and told us that she was sure we would do well there.

"These people love to eat," she said matter-of-factly, her mouth full of pretzel. We laughed and joked about that for weeks.

On the way home that night, Jonas drove Jake's little white van so that Jake could sit in the back and count the money. Cruising down I-283, Jake went through that day's sales, a whopping (to us at the time) $440. Everyone got so excited about that opening—here was a way that my brother could make almost $2,000 a month by working only four extra days. It's hard to believe, but that store is still open today, seventeen years later, selling pretzels every Saturday.

By the time the summer of 1989 rolled around, another one of my siblings was ready to open a store, and this time it was my brother Merrill, with the location being the Morgantown Farmers' Market in Morgantown, Pennsylvania. He and his wife partnered up with another couple we had known for years and prepared to start their own Auntie Anne's.

Once again we scouted out the potential locations together and sat down in a local diner to discuss the details. Merrill's wife, Verna, became one of my closest friends and confidants when we returned from Texas, and I was excited for them. Sitting there in that rinky-dink diner, we signed some hand-written papers that Jonas and I put together. (I can't remember our paperwork from those days, but the total contract, leasing agreement and licensing agreement was between one and three pages in length!)

During the next week or two, Jonas helped them build their location, find the equipment at used-equipment stores, and prepare for the opening. These days quickly became some of the most exciting of my life—with each store opening came the preparation, the build out, the wondering about how well it would do, and then finally the openings, which in those days all turned out to be great successes. Each store ran so well because the owners worked the store themselves, and the costs always stayed within a manageable level. You would think that with each new successful store, I would have become more and more confident, more and more content. But that's not how I felt at all.

With each store I actually became more and more stressed out about the fact that I was not in control. I would lie awake at night wondering so many things: Were they making the pretzels properly? Were they giving good customer service? Were they keeping their stores clean? I knew exactly how everyone made their pretzels, which stores made them too fat, which stores made them too skinny, which stores baked them too dark, and which stores took them out of the oven too soon.

I also became increasingly worried about the recipe: in those days, whenever we opened a new location, we gave the recipe to the owners—they would then go out each week and buy the necessary ingredients, mix the batches themselves, and make the pretzels. I felt that the people we gave stores to were very trustworthy, but with each new location we introduced countless people into the circle of those who knew the recipe. On one hand, I wasn't handling the worry well at all, sometimes nearly collapsing under the stress. On the other hand, an event that happened shortly thereafter taught us all about the importance of protecting the recipe.

A man I will call Frank approached Jonas and me early in 1989, a man with energy and charisma equaled only by the size of his frame, and he wanted to open an Auntie Anne's Soft Pretzels store. His excitement became contagious, and in good faith we agreed to help him open a location—up until this time we dealt mostly with family, a fact which probably caused us to act a little on the naive side. But he seemed like a nice guy and wanted to open a store in a good farmers' market, so we threw ourselves into the effort of helping him open.

I traveled with Frank to a Kmart to help him pick out some supplies that he needed.

"Here, take this," he said, handing me a $100 bill.

"Okay, thanks," I said, going into the store and picking out the things he would need.

I paid with his money and kept the change and the receipt. He waited for me just on the other side of the checkout, and I handed him the receipt along with the change.

"Oh, just keep the change," he said calmly.

As soon as those words slipped from his mouth, a red flag went up inside of me. I don't know if the way he said it caught my attention, or if it just seemed out of character for him. In any case, for some reason I knew I had to give him the change. It felt too much like a trap.

"No, really," I said. "I insist."

I gave him the change.

Later that week it came time to open Frank's location at the farmers' market. As far as I can remember, he did very well. He hired a group of Amish girls who worked very hard and learned quickly. I also remember that he served customers with some of the best customer service I had seen yet, and I walked away feeling pretty good about how he would run his store.

You can imagine my surprise when, after three or four weeks of his paying his 4 percent royalty religiously, the check didn't arrive. *Hmmm*, I thought to myself, *I wonder where Frank's check is?* Yet even with the absence of the royalty check, I could never have prepared myself for the phone call that came next.

"Hello?" I said, answering the phone that night in the kitchen of our house.

Frank was on the other end of the line, and he was furious. To this day I can't even remember what he was so angry about, but he just kept screaming and going off, shouting and hollering and making me very uncomfortable, mostly because he kept putting down Jonas and saying he hadn't done a very good job with the opening and building of the store. Immediately I felt flashbacks to the days when Pastor had a hold on my life— one of the first ways he tried to get at me was by putting down my husband. I started shaking, unable to control my emotions.

Finally I managed to squeak out a sentence.

"Frank, if you have a problem with Jonas, maybe we should all sit down together and talk about it."

Eventually we decided to meet at a restaurant and talk about it, but our meeting didn't do any good. After he left, Jonas and I just sat there in shock, not knowing what to say. It became fairly obvious that he was making a fuss so that he could get out of paying royalties, and we didn't have a written agreement that would stand up. We never received another royalty payment from Frank, and the confrontation with him was enough to make me want to give it all up, just stop with the stores we had already built. But Jonas wasn't putting up with that. Sure, we made a mistake when it came to Frank (who continued running his store), but that didn't mean we should just quit.

"There are two things we have to do," Jonas said. "First, we have to put an agreement together. And second, we have to 'secretize' this recipe of ours."

During the next few weeks, we met with an attorney and put together an eleven-page licensing agreement. While the recipe still needed to be "secretized" (as Jonas so famously referred to it), we had a new contract in place with which we could continue to expand, and our store total reached nine: the two that we owned in Downingtown and Harrisburg, plus seven licensed stores located in farmers' markets in Pennsylvania. I felt comfortable operating in farmers' markets; after all, that was where we got our start. And farmers' markets tended to be more laid back about the appearance of the store and the way it was run. Yet toward the end of the summer of 1989, a woman from our church started hounding me about trying a completely different location.

A shopping mall.

"You know, Anne, you really should let us open a location in the Park City Shopping Center. It's such a busy mall. We would sell so many pretzels there."

Something about her belief in the product resonated with my line of thinking at the time. I began seeing potential Auntie Anne's locations everywhere—not only markets but downtown locations, shopping centers, anywhere there was a lot of people, maybe even airports and train stations! I thought to myself, *What if we became like a McDonald's?* But as soon as the thought entered my mind, the more practical side of me would take over and I would think, *Maybe not. Probably not.*

But this woman was single-minded. She acted with complete determination, sure that she could open a location at Park City and do well. Finally I told her to go ahead and give it a try—if she could talk the management into letting us open in the mall, then she could have the location. I didn't think anything would come of it—she was a stay-at-home mom and didn't have any leasing connections or experience putting together rent-package proposals (neither did we, at that point, and we were far too busy to learn). A few weeks later I talked to her again.

"Well, I met with the mall manager at Park City, and he's

not going to let us come in, but I'm going to meet with him again," she said. I didn't have high hopes, to say the least.

She would take him pretzels and try to meet with him again and again. Finally at one point, after hearing of another failed attempt, I casually suggested that maybe she should just back off. It didn't appear that she was getting anywhere.

"Back off? No way. I am going to sell pretzels in Park City," she said with determination.

I never would have pushed that hard, and maybe if it was left to me, we never would have gone into shopping malls. One day in August or September, she came up to me at church with different news.

"Well," she said, "I've got a lease with Park City."

"You do?" I exclaimed.

"Yes, but they want us in before Thanksgiving."

Jonas already had his hands full building these other market locations, but if we were going to get into Park City, we had to do it before Thanksgiving. Normally two months would have been more than enough time to open a location, but normally we were opening in markets, not shopping malls. That Park City location became our first encounter with the real world of building regulations and fire regulations and architectural drawings. Inspectors and leases and fire marshals.

We finally met with the mall manager at the Park City Shopping Mall. He was a good old Southern boy from Arp, Texas, only ten minutes from the small town in Texas where we had lived. His Southern accent drawled out slowly, and he was firm.

"Ma'am," he had said, "I tell you what. I don't see how you can make your rents selling only pretzels. But I will let you in this shopping center—I don't really know why—and this is the only space I have available for you. You can stay for three months and then we'll see how it goes." The location was probably the worst one in the mall, a dark corner unit barely visible at the back of the food court. The mall manager didn't have very much belief in the product. In fact, he didn't think we would make it past the holidays.

Not a smart move for us to make with just a three-month lease in a horrible location, but we went ahead anyway, unable to imagine a situation in which we would not succeed. For one of the first times, I was in awe of what we were doing: the store looked great, very professional, and had a neon sign above the shiny, new equipment. It was the Cadillac of all our locations, and I thought we had arrived.

On grand opening day they sold pretzels faster than they could make them. Once again the product proved itself. They literally could not keep up, even with me and other family members there to help. And what of the doubting mall manager? Well, he went on to become one of our most beloved franchisees, opening four stores in Atlanta, our first stores in Georgia.

So there we were, Christmas of 1989. Park City sold an incredible number of pretzels during the holidays, and all of the market stands stayed busy. Our store total reached ten, and even without spending a cent on franchise marketing, more and more people would call each week asking if they could open an Auntie Anne's. By January 1990 we hired managers for our two stores, Downingtown and Broad Street, but I still tried to be at the stores on the weekends, and with our increasingly busy schedule, Jonas and I realized we simply could not keep up.

The main area in which we needed help was in the actual building of stores. As we began to look at locations that required a more professional appearance, we realized we could not open stores in the one-week time frame that we could open farmers' market locations. We built everything in the store, including the shelves, the walls, and the cabinets, all from scratch, and Jonas needed help. We decided to ask my brother-in-law Aaron, Becky's husband, if he would come on full-time and help Jonas with the build-out side of things.

Aaron worked for Stoltzfus Structures, a local shed-building company. We asked him if he wanted to be our first full-time "corporate" employee—I was nervous, though, because I didn't even know for sure if we could actually pay him every week. In spite of the uncertainty, there was an excitement in the air when it came to Auntie Anne's Soft Pretzels, and Aaron decided to take us up on our offer.

Meanwhile, Becky continued managing Downingtown for me and tagging along with Aaron during the weeks. The four of us would hang out all the time, trying to figure out how to do things better and talking about our existing licensees and who was doing a good job, who was struggling, who made the best pretzels, all of that kind of stuff. There was a little diner we met regularly, and my brother Merrill would often join us as we talked about the direction the company seemed to be headed.

We still struggled with the idea of "secretizing" the recipe. Eventually we decided to bag the mix ourselves and eliminate the need for the licensees to know the ingredients. We tried so many different strategies—from brown bags stapled shut to plastic bags fastened with a metal tie, then went through various boxes and containers to ship the mix to the store owners.

The whole process started around March, and I discovered my sister Becky was taking over more and more of the responsibility when it came to the packaging of the mix. She would work for hours at a stretch, making one bag of mix at a time, taking orders from the store owners who called, and even arranging for some of the younger nephews and nieces to come and help bag mix—I think we paid them 10 cents for each bag they put together. For those four months at the beginning of 1990, Becky worked as hard as the rest of us, never asking for an extra cent above what she got paid for managing Downingtown. Finally one day in April while we were bagging mix in my garage with one of my nephews, I turned to her and laughed.

"Becky, if you keep coming to work, I'm going to have to start paying you!"

She just laughed.

"You don't have to pay me. I'm just hanging around here with Aaron. I don't have anywhere else to be."

But we finally got to the place where I could pay her, and she became our second full-time employee. Once again my family was there for me, just jumping in as the need arose. I couldn't have done it without them. Their presence served as a continual reminder to me: even though I wanted to control the process and have everything done my way, I couldn't do it all on my own. I had to depend on them, and they were all very dependable.

During 1989 and the first few months of 1990, the business became an all-consuming whirlwind that just picked me up and never put me back down. By the end of 1989, we had already opened ten locations and sold over 200,000 soft pretzels. Jonas and my two girls were caught up in it as well, and we all had our own individual responses. Jonas continued counseling, growing that side of things exponentially, as well as building store after store for me. The girls, on the other hand, weren't doing well at all: LaWonna was never home, and LaVale became more and more withdrawn. There were still so many skeletons in my closet, too many past hurts and disappointments that I hadn't dealt with properly. The business served as a suitable Band-Aid for the time being, but at some point that Band-Aid would have to come off.

CHAPTER SEVEN

Graveside Confessions

When written in Chinese, the word "crisis" is composed of two characters: one represents danger, and the other represents opportunity.

—JOHN F. KENNEDY

I've traveled around the world visiting my pretzel stores in many places, from Thailand to the Philippines, from the east coast of the United States to the west coast, but no matter how many places I've visited, I still find Lancaster County, Pennsylvania, to be one of the most beautiful. A feeling rises up in me when I drive these old familiar roads lined with high-standing corn, when I see the farms spreading out in a long valley before me, when I smell freshly cut hay lying quietly on a summer's night.

It's good to be home, good to be back with Angie. I felt guilty when we lived in Texas, guilty that we left her lying there in the earth so far from where we moved. I visit her grave three or four times a year, and just recently I took my granddaughter Trinity, LaWonna's little girl, along for the visit. She rode quietly beside me in the car on the way, just the two of us—I'm not sure how much she understood at the time about Angie, but she is a thoughtful girl and I think she often catches on to more than we give her credit for. In the least she knew that her mother used to have a sister, but that sister is gone now.

I drove along those winding country roads, flashbacks jumping out at every corner. I could see my brother Jake's old trailer home where I sat with his wife, Shirl, and told her about my dreams and fears and how we prayed for peace. Just a bit farther along I see our trailer home, where we lived so happily up until that moment I heard the screaming. I wonder if they still have that old green telephone I reached for (I'm sure they don't); I wonder if the stones would still cut into my feet the way they did that day I ran down the lane, not knowing where to run.

Then there's the stone house my parents lived in, the barns still standing, the spot where Angie died looking like just another patch of driveway. I look down at Trinity and squeeze her hand. We keep driving, past more farms and through those old country road intersections, finally turning right and driving up to a small church. We park in the parking lot, and I remember how the cars lined the road on the day of Angie's funeral, parked halfway in the grassy banks to leave room for others to squeeze by.

The cemetery is a small one, running maybe a hundred yards along the road and ten to twelve grave plots deep with a little paved walkway down the middle. An immense green hill rises up behind us, the top of it covered in trees, and in front of us a long valley stretches out with hardly a house to be seen. It's a peaceful place, a perfect place to stop and rest. The day is calm, and a warm summer breeze floats around us.

Trinity and I walk together about two-thirds of the way down the cemetery, then turn left into the grass. I see my father's headstone, the dates of his life carved in granite, but when Angie died that stone wasn't there—he stood beside the rest of us, unable to fathom her passing. Angie's flat head-stone sits directly beside his, and Trinity and I sit down beside it. There's a large metal locket fastened onto Angie's grave-stone, and when I flip up the top, I see the picture of her we keep there. On the inside of the locket someone etched a mes-sage in long scratched letters: "It's okay, Aunt Fi."

For five or ten minutes I sit there, simply wondering what life would be like if Angie still lived with us, not in a bad way or even a sad way, but just thinking of the happy possibilities. Would she be married, have children? The questions come more from a constant curiosity than from any sort of anger or grief.

I also try to imagine, sometimes with even more difficulty, what I would be like today. What would have become of me dur-ing those twenty-five years if I hadn't lived with the despair that came with Angie's death? For a while I saw Angie's death as something that changed me in a way that should not have hap-pened, as a defining event that charted the course my life had taken. Angie's death was obviously a tragedy, so how could what became of my life be anything but a tragedy as well?

But I don't see it that way anymore. Now I see Angie's death more as an experience that taught me many things, and I can see how her death actually changed me for the good. When I see people going through pain and crisis, my heart breaks for them because I understand the loss they feel; but I also know they will go places they've never been, and if they remain open, they will find God in places they've never found him before. If I think about death, and Angie's death in particular, there is nothing positive about the naked fact of the death of a child. Whenever a child dies, it is a terrible loss. But these days I cannot think about the loss of Angie without thinking of the positive ways that God has changed me. It took me nearly thirty years, but in 2003 I spoke at a large gathering and found myself saying, rather unexpectedly, that I truly believed at that point that all things work together for the good of those who love God.

Trinity sat there on the grass beside me, her long hair blowing in a gentle breeze. She looked so much like her mother did at that age, not much older than her mother was when Angie died. "Thank you, Angie. Thank you for teaching me. Thank you for living with us for nineteen months and twelve days. Thank you for helping me become a better person."

Yet that's not how I always felt when I visited Angie's grave. During those first years, after Jonas and the girls and I moved north from Texas, returning to Pennsylvania, my visits to Angie's grave simply reminded me of my failings as a mother and a wife. As I mentioned earlier, I felt guilty for leaving her in Pennsylvania when we moved to Texas. I felt guilty that I couldn't protect her. I wanted to know the person she would have turned out to be, not in a peaceful, happy way, but in a way that led to despair and hopelessness. I rarely visited her in those days, and that's not surprising when I think of the way those visits made me feel.

Still the business continued to grow, and I sank deeper and deeper into the somewhat comforting clutches of busyness. Opening stores, supporting our small network of "licensees," visiting with potential new-store owners, searching for more locations . . . running Auntie Anne's became the gauze that fit perfectly over the seeping wound that was my soul.

I don't mean to make it all sound so heavy—mixed in with the stress and the activity came lots of fun times. By the end of 1990, we would have fifty Auntie Anne's locations in nine states. The days were exciting, thrilling, draining, busy, and absolutely crazy. My team consisted almost entirely of family members, and we had all grown up working hard, appreciating the feeling that came after a long day of giving it our best. I have so many positive memories from that summer, like the day Aaron drove off to the shore in a huge brown van dragging an overstuffed trailer. His mission: to open five shore-point locations. Or when LaWonna took over as trainer, teaching all new store owners the ropes. So many things took place that summer, it's no wonder Jonas and I felt the need to hire someone to oversee it all.

At some point Jonas and I finally sat down to talk about our organization. There were too many things to do between the two of us, our three new employees (Aaron, Becky, and my younger brother Merrill, who joined us early in the summer of 1990 as a deliveryman), and others who were helping on a part-time basis. We needed someone to step in and organize us, especially some of the financial areas. But we didn't know where to begin, where to look, or what to do to attract the right person.

Jonas came up with the idea of listing everything we needed this new person to do. "Fine," I said. "That makes sense." So we pulled out a lined sheet of yellow notebook paper and started writing: do accounting and bookkeeping work, manage the warehouse, oversee and develop contracts, provide direction in supporting our stores, introduce new products, help develop processes for everything from mixing a batch of dough to opening a new store . . . the list went on and on. Finally we finished and said a prayer together, trusting that God would bring us the right person.

Initially there was one friend we considered for the post, but she wasn't from Lancaster County, something that at the time made us a little nervous. Would a complete stranger to our area understand our culture enough to create a positive working relationship? How would this person ever fit perfectly into a role that required so many different strengths and areas of knowledge? Finally, what would it be like to work with, and give so much responsibility to, someone who wasn't family?

Then in July of 1990 everything fell into place. My youngest brother, Carl, approached Jonas and me and said he would like to meet with us over a cup of coffee. We met with him, and you can imagine our surprise when he said he wanted to work with us at Auntie Anne's. *Hmmm*, I thought to myself, *I didn't think of Carl as being the person to oversee things*. He started going over the various areas where he thought he could contribute, and his verbal list nearly matched our written one word for word. When I got home, I pulled out that sheet of yellow notebook paper and realized that Carl mentioned every major point. He could do everything we were looking for. Jonas and I called Carl back, and he joined us in August.

One day around the time that Carl joined us, I answered the phone in our little house and was greeted by a voice belonging to the boyfriend of one of our licensees.

"Hi, Anne," he said, and then he introduced himself. "There's something important I need to talk to you about. I'm not sure if you have the right business model, and you might find yourself in some trouble."

Suddenly I got very concerned. I had flashbacks to the problems we'd already experienced with Frank. What was I doing wrong? Why did I keep ending up with these troublemakers? I met him at a restaurant, and we sat in the second booth on the left in the old dining room.

He started by telling me his background.

"I used to be involved in a franchise," he said. "And I know what a franchise looks like. You call yourself a licensor, but I don't think you're licensing. The way you are running your business, I'm pretty sure it's more of a franchising model. You really should look into it."

"But we've got lawyers who drew up all our agreements," I said, "and they seem to think we *are* licensing."

"I'm not trying to cause trouble, Anne," he said. "But I will tell you one thing: you are franchising. You need to talk to a franchising attorney and have them draw up a disclosure document. If you don't have that, you could get into some trouble, maybe even a fine—I don't know."

Jonas and I left that meeting feeling completely overwhelmed. At least I was. To this day I am so thankful he brought it up with me, but at the time I immediately felt discouraged by the prospects of what lay ahead. Were we doing something illegal? Would I get into trouble? I just wanted to sell soft pretzels and help other people do the same thing—how expensive would it be to change from licensing to franchising? Could the business survive my mistake?

Jonas, as usual, encouraged me, saying we would do what we had to do to keep the company going. I also bought a book that talked about the more technical aspects of franchising, how it differed from licensing. The more I read, the more I felt that, yes, this is what we were doing! I knew we needed to make the change, which meant finding someone who knew what they were doing, someone who could help us through the process. I also felt that we couldn't make such a fundamental change while still opening stores at that frenetic pace, averaging nearly a store a week. I met with my fledgling organization, which now consisted of my brother-in-law Aaron (full-time store builder and fine tuner), my sister Becky (helped with just about everything but seemed to be specializing in taking orders and overseeing the production of our mix), my brother Merrill (part-time deliveryman), my brother Carl (given the monumental task of organizing our headstrong, motley crew), and my husband, Jonas (busy building a nonprofit counseling organization as well as helping build a business). Together we tried to create a plan that would help us move forward.

Carl made an important connection with a company called Francorp, which helps franchisors get started. As he talked to them, we realized more and more that we were in fact franchising and needed to make some major changes to get on the right track. This was in the fall of 1990, and the responsibility felt heavier and heavier with each passing day.

Meanwhile, things at home continued to get more and more difficult. Sure, there was the "normal" chaos around the house that resulted from owning a growing business: our butter in the fridge was in one-pound blocks as opposed to sticks; retired market towels made their way into our kitchen for a few more weeks of use before being thrown away; money wrappers and coin rolls and bank bags cluttered more than one countertop; hard chunks of "washed" pretzel dough clogged the clothes dryer; generic plastic shopping bags with the words *Thank You* on the front doubled as small trash can liners.

Unfortunately, the chaos spread to our family's emotional life as well. LaWonna still hung out with the same group of friends, and I worried more and more about her as the months passed. LaWonna and her boyfriend always spent time at his house with his parents, and never at our house with Jonas and me, causing me to feel rejected. One of the lowest points of those years with LaWonna came when a picture of her boyfriend showed up in the paper—he had been arrested. I felt humiliated and became furious with her for even associating with him.

Then there was LaVale. She, too, seemed to slip away from me. She was so young, so innocent—we had been such good pals! But she spent more and more time with LaWonna. At first I felt good about their times together because it made our family feel more cohesive, even though it didn't necessarily involve me. But soon I started to see that her time with LaWonna only exposed her to things a fourteen-year-old shouldn't be exposed to, shouldn't see firsthand. My realization came too late, though, and soon I began to see LaVale following all the same paths LaWonna had taken. With complete despair I once again felt my family was falling apart, and no amount of success in the business world could make up for it.

At some point during those months, LaVale, Jonas, and I decided it might be a good idea for her to get some counseling, just meet with someone she felt comfortable speaking with, someone she could trust. She started meeting with the pastor at our church on a regular basis, trying to work through some things. In spite of my experience with pastoral counseling, I didn't worry about her meeting with our pastor (he was a childhood friend), and I was happy she wanted to look for help. But a small part of me still felt disappointed that she couldn't just talk to me about her problems.

A few weeks after LaVale began her counseling sessions, I approached our pastor just to see how things were going.

"Well," he said, "I can tell you that LaVale is very troubled."

Immediately I was concerned.

"What do you mean, troubled? I know she's been struggling with depression recently, but is it something she can work through?"

"She's very upset," he cautioned me. "She feels like she's living under a cloud. She feels that there's a secret that everyone but her knows. She feels disconnected from the family."

Up until that point I had not spoken with LaVale about the things that had happened with Pastor for those six long years. During the late eighties and early nineties, I still viewed what had happened between him and me as an affair for which I was totally to blame—it wasn't until meeting with a counselor that I realized how he had abused his power as well as my vulnerability after losing Angie. Jonas and I often talked about when the right time would be to tell LaVale, but she always seemed too young or too angry. I thought that telling her would only shatter any remaining relationship I had with her, that she wouldn't be able to understand, or that she would hate me for being unfaithful to her father.

Back in 1982, when I broke the silence and revealed my secret, I felt the need to tell LaWonna what had happened—she was eleven years old at the time and I didn't know if I could explain the nature of what had happened to me, but I felt that she might hear it through the grapevine, and I wanted her to hear it from me first. Back then I knew very little about the effects a confession like that could have on a child. During the whole discussion LaWonna just sat there, listening very intently. I could tell she understood me very well.

Soon after our talk she handed me a letter:

Mom,

   Thanks for telling me! Please don't think I'm angry with you cause I'm not. I love you more than I ever did. Don't even think I'll hold it against you cause I won't. If the Lord has the heart to forgive you, so do I.

Love ya bunches,
LaWonna Lynn

P.S. I would have told you this myself, but I know I would cry!

CASE CLOSED
Don't ever bring the subject up again! Please. I love you.

❖

"Do you think I should tell LaVale about Pastor?" I asked our new preacher.

He paused.

"I don't know," he concluded. "If you tell her, it could devastate her. If you don't tell her, and she finds out from someone else, she could lose all trust in you. You are in a difficult spot, Anne. I can't see either road being easy."

But that's what I wanted, an easy road!

After long talks and deliberations, Jonas and I decided to tell LaVale about the things in my past. I just felt that even though she seemed so young, she was bound to find out about it from someone in the community. After all, everyone else knew about it. So one sunny afternoon I got in the car with LaVale and LaWonna and set out for Angie's grave. It was the only place on earth I thought I could reveal my secret.

❖

Meanwhile, the business grew out of control. Totally out of control. Every single week that summer we raced to a store opening, including numerous shore-point locations. When word of Park City's success began to spread, more shopping mall locations became available. Farmers' markets continued opening as well. We were growing outside of Pennsylvania, trusting more and more store owners to uphold our high standards of cleanliness, customer service, and the creation of the best pretzel known to man. We moved into our first main office and built a training center with a warehouse in the back. And then there was the licensing versus franchising issue. By the end of 1990, we would have fifty locations open in nine different states, and we ended up selling over 800,000 pretzels.

Finally during one of our meetings, Carl made the bold statement "Maybe we should stop opening stores until the end of spring, next year."

We all just kind of sat around and looked at each other. How in the world would we do that? It sounded like the right thing to do, but the phone rang off the hook every day with more and more people wanting to open an Auntie Anne's location. And then there were the existing franchisees, most of whom experienced tremendously successful locations and wanted to open number two, number three, number four. It always amazed me to see how someone could go from being skeptical about the chances of success for a store that sold only pretzels to being desperate, nearly crazed, with the desire to open as many stores as we would allow them to open. The company snowballed into this gigantic force, and now someone proposed that we just stand in front of it with our hand up and say, "Stop"?

Amazingly enough, that is what we decided to do. Even though we needed cash, and every new opening represented that much-needed injection, even though the interest continued to grow, even though we had dear friends begging us to let them open a store, we decided to say stop. Carl was the driving force behind that decision—I never could have made that decision on my own. I was too interested in pleasing people, and I could only see all of the people who would be upset by such a strategy—I didn't want to be the one to tell them. Carl, on the other hand, could see that if we continued building stores at that pace, the wheels would come off. We just couldn't sustain that kind of growth. We needed to stop, catch our breath, get organized, and create some systems before moving ahead.

All that remained was telling the franchisees. We decided to make the announcement at the next gathering: the Christmas banquet.

LaWonna, LaVale, and I stepped out of the car at the small Mennonite church and walked the narrow paved path to Angie's grave. I could feel the emotion welling up inside of me already and clutched tighter to a piece of paper in my hand. LaVale and LaWonna were both very serious, probably wondering what in the world I was doing.

"I brought you here," I told LaVale, "because I wanted to tell you something. But it's very hard for me to talk about. So I brought this for you to read. This should tell you pretty much everything you need to know."

I handed LaVale an old bulletin from our church in Texas. On the back of it was a picture of Jonas and me. Under the picture someone had written a few paragraphs about our availability to serve as marriage counselors for couples struggling to keep their marriage together. The text also provided a very brief history, explaining what had happened with Pastor and how marriage counseling helped Jonas and me stay together.

All this time LaWonna sat off to the side, waiting. She knew my history and had known for years. I wanted to know what she thought about it, how she felt toward me, but I didn't say anything. I just stared at LaVale and waited for the storm.

As LaVale's fourteen-year-old eyes scanned down the page, I could see the color drain from her face. As she finished reading, I expected screaming, raging, crying. I expected her to scorn me and walk away. What I did not expect was for her to look at me with icy green eyes and ask one question.

"Is Daddy really my daddy?"

"Of course Daddy is your daddy," I protested, the tears flowing. How I hated those tears and the emotional weakness they signified to me. I wanted to hold it all together. I wanted to stay strong. I didn't want to be the one always breaking down. Yet there I was, sobbing when I felt I should be the one consoling my daughter.

That day was a turning point in many ways. For me it became the day I finally felt free of that horrible secret, although I wouldn't feel the relief of that release for a long time because of the circumstances surrounding my confession. For LaVale, though, I think that afternoon was a slap in the face, the inevitable strike that comes when someone learns that everyone around them has been "in the know." Up until that point I think she saw the trials our family experienced as relatively everyday sorts of trials: a little spat here, a disagreement there. But when I told her about my past, I think it put everything into question for her; the very nature of our family and our history was suddenly cast into doubt. Even her own identity seemed a mirage.

From that day on, the bond between LaVale and LaWonna became permanent. They spent summers at the beach together, ran off together for days at a time. They went to parties together and got into trouble together. I think the knowledge of my past mistakes served as a strong bond between them. They were in a common rebellion, and the upcoming years would prove to be almost more than I could bear.

❖

I sat at one of the tables in a local restaurant with Jonas, Carl, Becky, and Aaron, along with some of my other main employees. We were surrounded by more than one hundred people, licensees and their families. It was Christmas of 1990, one of our first company-wide meetings, and there we sat, preparing to tell them the company they loved was going to stop growing for about six months.

Thankfully, Carl made the announcement.

He told them that we weren't going to do any more new deals for a little while. If they were at the banquet and we had already agreed a deal with them, we would move forward with that, but outside of existing locations we were putting growth on hold. Completely.

A lot of people were very upset. It was during this time that a few franchisees attempted to tie up larger territories, something we shied away from, preferring to allocate each store one at a time, location by location. Franchisees from Baltimore, New York, and New Jersey pressed for the rights to develop those areas—they were concerned with competition coming in and taking the prime locations, one of my main concerns as well, but I just knew we could not continue to grow in that helter-skelter way.

In the end most of our franchisees understood our decision and respected us for making it. And we probably did lose some locations during that time. Yet we needed the time to clarify our vision, organize our efforts, and restructure our system around franchising versus licensing. We often found that out of our greatest frustrations came our greatest advances. Our frustration with poorly performing units led to the assembly of better agreements up front as well as increased training and support. Our frustration with our licensing issue led to an exploration of the franchising community, where we learned many crucial lessons from companies that went before us.

But blinded by the frustration, I couldn't see or appreciate the advances we were making. As the weeks passed and we entered that difficult period of remaking ourselves in early

1991, I continued down farther and farther. Every difficult business moment became a crisis in my head, until I didn't feel I could go any farther.

Finally one day I entered our small office and sat down at my four-foot-by-five-foot cubicle (my desk barely fit into the space allotted). I prepared to visit a problem licensee in another state: the product there was very disappointing. I couldn't believe how horribly some people could make my wonderful pretzel! I gathered my things together and tried to get psyched up before making the three-hour drive to visit with this difficult person. I just kept thinking, *There is no way I can get through this day.*

Carl came up to my cubicle and let me know he'd scheduled a meeting with an outside company to work on our training manuals. That was one of Carl's main projects (of many) during those months, and he did a good job finding outside resources to help us expedite the process.

"Just wanted to let you know the meeting is in a few days," he said.

"Okay," I said, but just as he turned to go, I couldn't hold the emotions in any longer. There were too many people to see, too many places to go, too many projects to think about, and I felt it physically impossible to stretch myself any further. All of my energy literally drained out of me, and I collapsed from my chair onto the floor, almost fainting in exhaustion.

Becky came running.

"What's wrong, Anne? Are you okay?"

My brother Merrill was also in the office, and he joined Carl in racing over to my side. I couldn't stop crying.

"What's wrong?" they asked.

At first I couldn't speak. Finally I gasped a few words.

"I don't know. I don't know what's wrong."

"What can we do?" Becky asked.

"I just can't go on," I said. "There's just too much."

"But we'll help you," they said.

There they stood, my brothers and my sister without whom I could not have started the business. They were such a support to me. At first they suggested that they take me to the hospital to make sure I was okay, but I turned them down.

"I'm fine," I said, sitting there on the floor of our offices. I wasn't fine, but I had trouble admitting to myself that something was wrong. I felt I had to push on.

So a little while later I was on the road, driving to New Jersey. I cried the whole way, sure I was going to lose my mind. The business controlled every aspect of my life, and I felt certain that it would destroy me.

CHAPTER EIGHT

Surviving Prosperity

The human race has had long experience and a fine tradition
in surviving adversity. But we now face a task for which we
have little experience: the task of surviving prosperity.

—ALAN GREGG

During the early days of the company, from the opening of our second location through 1993 and 1994, my life, along with the lives of my girls, seemed completely out of control. My own anger and frustration, for one, filled me to the point where grace could not find a niche, not even the smallest little cranny. My inward struggles formed the core of my difficulties, whether it be my insecurity as a business leader or my feelings of inadequacy as a mother and wife. Eventually I could see that these internal battles led me into a time of personal growth like nothing I had ever experienced before. At these times I felt God testing me, pushing me, stretching me, and while at many points I could not deal emotionally with the stress that came from this intense molding, it had to happen. The adversity had to take place or I would not become the person I needed to be in order to fulfill my calling.

Most of the time, even during those rare moments when I recognized how necessary these trials were, I still didn't like going through them.

During those years in the company we brought on many good people from outside the family, people who filled specific roles, people who strengthened our position as a company. But I still felt the heavy weight of responsibility for the success of the company, the employees, and the franchisees, no matter how many specialists we brought in. I knew that I needed to be a good steward of our resources, and in that area I felt most tested.

Seeing my name everywhere, having people recognize our accomplishments, always being in the spotlight: these things started to challenge my integrity. In those early days of success, when it started to look as though we could take the company far, my pride and vanity became the testing ground. I didn't want to get some kind of elevated view of myself—I still wanted to see myself as little Anne Smucker running barefoot down our dirt lane, or baking pies in the basement, or ice skating on a cold winter's night. But sometimes it was difficult. At times I got caught up in the whole illusion of Auntie Anne, the illusion that everyone knew me and my company. Everywhere I turned I found people focused only on my success, giving me a false sense of who I was.

Yet I constantly tried to remind myself that this company was not about me. It was about God and his plan. It became a difficult road to walk, and, ironically enough, it wasn't until I conquered myself in 1998 or 1999 that the path became straighter and I began to find a peace that wasn't twisted and bashed around by every little circumstance. In that year of 1999, I came out of something that is more embarrassing to me than anything else I've done in my life, yet through it I came to understand myself better. The anger I held inside of me had to be diffused. My incessant need to be in complete control had to be tamed. And after I surrendered in 1999, I finally stopped fighting.

In *God Calling*, A. J. Russell writes that "in order to conquer adverse circumstances, one must conquer themselves." This amazes me, because whenever I felt most vulnerable, I would blame it on the circumstances around me: my girls getting into trouble, Jonas and I not connecting, my business stressing me out. But the whole time it was me! It was my self that needed conquering, my pride and self-reliance and need to be in control. Those were the real problems. But I didn't see that. The only thing I could see were the various areas of my life that seemed to be crumbling around me.

❖

During the spring of 1991, I encountered a serious problem: LaVale refused to go to school. She was fourteen, turning fifteen in the fall, and I physically could not make her go to school. I would wake her up in the morning and she would go back to sleep. I would literally help her out of bed, but she would just sit there. If I managed to get her in the car and to the front of the school, I would later discover that she never went inside. The absent days began mounting up, and I doubted that she would even pass the ninth grade.

She wouldn't come home until late, well after midnight. We set curfews, but they were useless. I didn't know it at the time, but she began drinking heavily and even dabbling in drugs. Finally I got to the point where I had absolutely no control over her. She was in ninth grade! Devastated, I didn't know what to do.

Finally I decided that if she would not go to school, I would bring the school to her. I decided to homeschool LaVale, which we did for her tenth-grade year. We hired a tutor to help her with her classes—I was entirely unequipped to teach tenth grade (I didn't go to school beyond eighth grade), and besides that I had no spare time. I did drive her to a local college once a week to see another tutor, and as the year passed she got good grades. But LaVale has always been an intelligent girl: the homeschooling thing was too easy for her, and it accommodated her lifestyle of staying out late, partying, and sleeping until noon. I knew homeschooling couldn't last because eventually she would lose interest. But I didn't know what else to do.

❖

Meanwhile, the company continued growing. By May 1992 we were receiving calls from all over the country, nearly daily, from people who wanted to open a store in their shopping mall. California, Washington, Texas, Florida: you name the place, we had potential franchisees. But we wanted to grow strategically, and soon we found ourselves saying over and over again: "I'm sorry, but we're not opening in that area. Please give us your details and we will contact you when we are ready."

It got frustrating, but we just couldn't line up enough locations for the crazy number of potential franchisees. Then one day a franchisee came to us.

"You guys have to go to the ICSC in Vegas. Honestly, if you

would go there, you would get so many locations you wouldn't know what to do with them."

The whole idea of having enough locations everywhere in the country to meet the growing list of potential franchisees sounded very appealing.

"What's the ICSC?"

"The International Council of Shopping Centers. Every major developer goes there to check out new concepts. You should do an Auntie Anne's information booth there. I'm telling you, at least look into it. It is a huge show and can be very difficult to get into, but at least give them a call."

So Carl called, and once again his persistence and determination made a difference in the path our company was about to take. Initially the response of the people at ICSC seemed positive. They had one location left, and they sent us a packet of information.

"This is ridiculous," Carl said after looking it over. "Do you see where they are putting us? That is the far back corner of the convention hall. No one will see us. We need a better location."

So he called the woman back from the ICSC registration office and told her we needed a better place in the hall.

"I'm sorry," she said. "Those central locations are reserved for years in advance. That's the only remaining place we have for this year's convention."

"Well," Carl said, "call me back if a better location opens up."

Oh well, we thought to ourselves, that year's ICSC was less than six weeks away, and we would have been pushing it to have everything ready in time. But in a few days, the ICSC called back.

"I can't believe this," the same woman said. "But a location opened up right in the middle of the convention center. It's one of the best locations we have."

They sent us another packet of information, and it was true. In fact, the location that they wanted to give us was only a few locations away from Carl's ideal spot. But Carl wasn't through.

He called that poor woman back.

"Ma'am, we really can't take a spot unless we are able to give away pretzels. No one knows what a pretzel tastes like, and if we can't give them away, there's no point in us being there."

"I'm sorry, sir," she said firmly. "No one gives product out. I don't even think you can get connected to water or the amount of electricity you would need."

"Okay," Carl said. "Then I guess we can't take the spot."

"Fine, fine," the woman replied. "Let me make some calls. I'll see what I can do. You guys sure are persistent!"

Within a few days we had an entirely new problem on our hands: building a store in four weeks that we could ship out to Vegas for the show. We needed all of the equipment and a team of motivated people. They said we could make soft pretzels right there in the convention hall. We were on top of the world.

We arrived in Vegas ready to take on the world and became the hit of the show that year. We gave away ten thousand free soft pretzels to developers and potential franchisees, working that small store with ten people, all of us moving as fast as we could. The ovens cranked, the rollers rolled pretzels, and that team proved to be one of the best ever assembled.

I say we, but actually I spent most of my time in the meeting room, telling our story over and over again to people who had never even heard of a soft pretzel before, let alone Auntie Anne's Soft Pretzels. Many of the people I met with started out with a lot of skepticism, much like the first mall manager we ran into at Park City Mall in Pennsylvania. But we just kept giving them product, and with one taste of the cinnamon-sugar soft pretzel, they were hooked. Once again, that incredible product just sold itself, but this time it was selling locations.

I remember walking through the aisles of that convention hall between meetings, feeling very nervous about how I looked. I didn't want to look like a country girl—I wanted to look credible, professional, businesslike. I even bought two new suits for myself before the meeting. But in many ways I still felt very out of place: as I walked those long corridors, it seemed that I encountered only men.

"What does it feel like to be a woman in a man's world?" some people have asked me throughout the years.

"It feels very much like the world I grew up in," I've always said. "I had five brothers." And it's true: I grew up comfortable around guys—in my family they made up the majority. But I think it also instilled in me a very competitive spirit. I always wanted to do things just as well as they did, and I always wanted to make the main man in my life, my dad, happy with whatever I did.

And so the week went. Meeting after meeting after meeting. More and more people totally impressed by what we did. Offers of locations began pouring in even before we left, and it took us weeks to organize all of the potential spots, as well as field all of the questions that flooded us after our first appearance at the ICSC. Seventy-five locations per year suddenly seemed very attainable.

❖

After the ICSC I returned home to find things generally unchanged: LaWonna still involved with people I didn't approve of; LaVale scraping by in her homeschool classes, getting good grades but still getting into trouble; and Jonas and me in a relationship that just couldn't quite get off the ground. Returning to the same old circumstances always seemed to disappoint me somehow: I guess I hoped that when I went away everyone would have profound revelations and change their lives to fit exactly what I wanted, but it never happened. Surprise, surprise. It just meant that whenever I got home I became more and more disillusioned with home life and tried to stay busier and busier with other things.

But ignoring the facts didn't make things much easier. Going into that summer of 1992, I knew that LaVale needed to go back to school. Homeschooling was beginning to wear on her, and while at first it may have carried some kind of novelty factor, by that summer I could tell she was through with it. I began dreading the fall, trying to get her to come back from the shore where she spent a lot of time with her sister, knowing I would have to convince her to start school again.

Jonas and I prayed a lot together about LaVale, asked God for some kind of wisdom, some idea. But nothing materialized. The weeks passed, and soon I found myself at the end of another busy summer. I knew LaVale should be getting ready for school, but she wasn't having any of it. The rather straightforward hints I dropped only brought old conflicts to the surface.

Finally I did something I'd never done before: I called one of those Christian Broadcasting Network prayer lines.

"Hello," a kind voice answered. "What can I pray with you about?"

"Hi, I'm having trouble with my daughter," I said, my voice trembling. "I don't know what to do. We can't discipline her in any way, and she's totally out of control."

I paused, not sure what to pray for, almost as if a solid mental wall separated me from any kind of understanding as to exactly what it was that LaVale needed.

"We need a miracle," I concluded.

That kind woman prayed with me for a little while over the phone, and I cried. Funny how when we pray for miracles, it doesn't take us long to start putting God into a box: fairly soon I formed an idea of exactly what God was going to do for us. LaVale's attitude would completely change, we would be at peace, and she would miraculously decide to respect us and go to bed at 9:00 and do all of her homework and stop hanging out with the wrong crowd. I guess God had other ideas. Two weeks later my miracle arrived.

❖

During the same time that I prayed for a miracle in LaVale's life, God accomplished a miracle in the life of my company: we opened our 100th location. The date was August 14, 1992, and the place was Granite Run Mall in Media, Pennsylvania.

I could hardly believe what that opening represented: our 100th store. If someone would have told me only three years earlier that I would open one hundred Auntie Anne's locations, I would have laughed in their face and told them, "Impossible." How can you accomplish something so remarkable without even having it as a goal? But God was in control and always had larger goals for the company than I did.

But by the time that store in Media opened, we felt we could do just about anything, open as many stores as we wanted, pretty much everywhere. The ICSC lay just behind us, and mall developers seemed desperate to have us. I won the Entrepreneur of the Year Award from Inc. Magazine, yet another thing about which to feel completely amazed. So much came together that year.

When I cut the blue ribbon hanging across the front of the store, I found myself whooping and hollering, I was so excited. Carl and Beck and many of our key employees were there, and I floated on this air of accomplishment and happiness. Many times successes such as that were the only things keeping me going.

There's another franchisee from that time that I want to tell you about: Janelle Byler. A beautiful young girl with brown hair and brown eyes as well as a friend of LaWonna's, she was one of our very first employees outside of family at Downingtown. For the first few years that she worked with us, even though she was only eighteen, all she could talk about was owning her own Auntie Anne's franchise. Did I mention her determination? By the way she used to fly around that Downingtown store, you would have thought she already owned it.

We couldn't stop her, even if we wanted to, and by the age of twenty-one she owned her own location in Echelon, New Jersey. Her happiness knew no bounds, and she was so bubbly and enthusiastic that the customers couldn't help but fall in love with her. Our youngest franchisee, and definitely one of our best, she had a presence about her that made her extremely lovable as well as successful.

LaWonna and Janelle formed a tight bond during those years, opening stores together and training people before Janelle had her own store. But even after Janelle became a franchisee, she would drop anything for LaWonna, for any of us really, if we needed her help or encouragement. Even after LaWonna opened a store of her own, the two of them managed to find time to be together. They were always helping each other out.

One Saturday night Jonas and I sat in our bed. I was reading and Jonas was studying when the phone rang. It was Janelle's parents.

Janelle was driving down to LaWonna's store in Ocean City, Maryland, to help her out—LaWonna was in New York training a new franchisee—when Janelle's car crossed the median and hit a truck head-on. Janelle was gone. Her parents called us to say they were heading down to identify her.

Would we please break the news to LaWonna?

I hung up the phone, then picked it up to call LaWonna. I held the phone in my hand for nearly an hour, just hurting for Janelle's parents, not wanting LaWonna to know. I knew I had to tell her, but I also knew the news would devastate her. So I sat there holding the phone, not knowing what to do. I would dial her number, then push down the button and hang up. Finally Jonas took the phone from my hand.

"We'll fly up in the morning," he said. "We'll fly up and tell her ourselves."

Early the next morning Jonas found someone to fly him and LaVale up to Messina, New York, in a private plane. They walked slowly into the shopping mall and found the Auntie Anne's store, all new and shiny and sparkling. LaWonna came out of the back room, already working hard, already starting her day. She buzzed around the store, motivating the employees and making the coffee. Then she looked up and saw her daddy, and at first her eyes lit up.

"Daddy!" she said.

But it only took her a fraction of a second to see the sadness in his eyes.

"Daddy. Who died? Daddy, who died?" and she nearly collapsed.

Jonas ran into the store and held her.

That was a tough moment in many ways. LaWonna lost a best friend. Janelle's parents lost their daughter. For our young company, it was like a punch in the stomach: so many exciting things had been happening, and we felt so invincible. After all, we were going to the top and no one could stop us. Janelle was the young franchisee bucking the odds to start her own successful business in the same way that we as a company were defying the odds. In some way, Janelle was us. Then Janelle died. We felt so broken. For months our spark was gone and sadness hung around the office.

Janelle was only twenty-two.

❖

It was a summer of highs and lows: attending the ICSC, opening our 100th location, and winning Entrepreneur of the Year were like mountaintops; losing Janelle led us back to rock bottom. By the end of that summer, the last thing I wanted to deal with was LaVale and her schooling. But I had to do something, so I called that prayer line.

One day I got home from work, and LaVale came into the kitchen.

"Mom," she said, "I'm going to finish school, but I'm moving away."

I was so surprised I couldn't say a thing. Going back to school? Moving away?

"I also know that you and Dad were going to make me go to

a Christian school, so I chose Eastern Mennonite High School in Virginia."

I didn't know what to say. Even though I didn't recognize it right away, this was the miracle I'd prayed for.

"We don't have enough time," I finally sputtered out. "It's the end of August. School starts any day."

"It's okay," LaVale said matter-of-factly. "I talked to the administrators today. They said there's an opening, and I just need my mom or dad to call in and make it official."

I must have looked pretty silly, trying to come up with various reasons why it wouldn't work for her to go to boarding school. She had thought through everything and there were no holes in her plan.

"Well, LaVale," I stammered, "what if I don't want you to move away? That's a good four-hour drive from here."

Suddenly her businesslike demeanor softened, and I could see a vulnerability creep into her eyes.

"Mom, I can't go back to the same old school. The same old friends. I have to get out of here."

I made the call, and in less than two weeks, we were driving her to her new school. On the way home, I cried my eyes out as Jonas drove. I never thought she would leave home so early, and I was scared she would attract the same old crowd. She did, and in some ways the same old troubles continued, but there was something about that school that kept her goodness very close to the surface.

Years later I went back to thank the principal for watching out for my daughter. LaVale once told me that he had kept her on the straight and narrow at times just because of the way he treated her with respect—every time he saw her in the hallway, he said hello and greeted her by name.

Her first year went fast, and in 1993 she enrolled again, this time for her senior year. Would she actually graduate? Would she pull herself out of the mess she had created? I could only watch and wait.

CHAPTER NINE

The Red Light

Zeal without knowledge is not good;
a person who moves too quickly may go the wrong way.

—PROVERBS 19:2 NLT

LaVale came home from her boarding school for Christmas 1993, and of course I couldn't restrain myself from launching into new sessions of worrying about her: Did she eat enough? Was she getting into trouble we didn't know about? Was the school strict enough to keep her in line? So many thoughts, so many concerns. Two days before Christmas, Jonas and I took her out for coffee, just to talk, and somehow we ended up arguing with her about how she didn't keep her room clean enough! How petty! All I wanted to do was hug her and tell her how much I loved her, but the only things that came out were more criticism and disagreement. The wedge between us seemed firmly driven in, and I couldn't do anything but build more walls to separate us.

One night during that Christmas season, my extended family piled into three or four vans and traveled from hospital to hospital in Lancaster County, walking through the halls and singing Christmas carols. The sound of our voices ringing through the halls brought many people out from their rooms: visitors dressed in warm clothes spending the holidays at the bedside of a relative; patients in those wispy gowns pulling IVs along behind them; older folks smiling and wishing us a merry Christmas. For those few hours I could forget about my own problems and be thankful for our health, our family. I listened to the thirty or so voices that formed our choir and felt blessed to have such a supportive family.

An entry from my journal at the end of 1993:

This is nearly Christmas 1993. I will journal from now on; I only regret I didn't start this five years ago when God started taking us one day at a time into the business called Auntie Anne's. What a journey it has been! I look back and marvel at how God has led us and how faithful he has been to us. Right now, it seems like I'm struggling with which way to go with the business. Do I need to continue the way we are financially with Jonas and I as sole owners, or is God opening my mind to new ideas? Do we need to go outside our little circle of thinking? Would it be the right thing to do to have private investors become a part of our business? At one point I never would have even considered it . . .

Christmas came and went, and we entered the first few weeks of January. No snow—just a firm coldness that went straight to your bones. LaVale returned to school, Jonas to the busy task of running a counseling center, and me, well, I was back in the full swing of running a business. The first order of 1994 was getting some product shots of our pretzels so we could better develop our marketing materials, and we found a firm in Atlanta to help us through the process.

While I went to Atlanta feeling down, I returned ready for the new year, energized and excited. Two days after I got back, we did the ribbon cutting ceremony at our new office building, and it turned out to be a huge success. More than one hundred visitors toured our new facilities. We had Dr. Richard Dobbins, founder of EMERGE Ministries, say a few words and spend the night with us. Becky and Aaron joined us for dinner, and our small group laughed until our stomachs hurt! It was my first meaningful encounter with Dr. Dobbins—how could I ever have imagined the impact he would have on my life in the coming years?

Jonas and I spent hours talking with him about how he grew EMERGE, the paths he took to get where he was, and the difficulties he faced. While EMERGE is a very different organization from Auntie Anne's, his wisdom on growing any type of organization proved valuable to us. And his personal counseling skills helped prepare me for the next few years, a time that would become the darkest in my life since Angie's death.

But some happy moments still remained. On May 25 a Christian television program called and asked if I would make an appearance. On one hand, the invitation thrilled me, and I couldn't wait; on the other hand, I knew they would be asking me about my past, the mistakes I made as well as the success I experienced, and that made me very nervous.

About two weeks after that invitation came an even more momentous occasion—LaVale graduated from high school! Nearly our entire extended family drove down to Harrisonburg, Virginia, to witness the event, an outpouring of support I knew LaVale appreciated. As I sat there watching LaVale accept her diploma, I was once again reminded of God's faithfulness to us—through all of the dark memories and difficult times, she made it. I was sure that from then on things with LaVale would be much better, much easier, and maybe even the relationship between the two of us would improve.

During that summer Jonas and I went with Aaron and Becky on a five-and-a-half-week motorcycle trek to the Black Hills in South Dakota. Increasingly I found solace on those long journeys when it was just me and the road and mile after mile of thinking time. With gorgeous scenery passing us on both sides, and occasional stops to eat or rest, the trip gave me some much-needed time away from the business, which in turn gave me even more confidence in my management team and their ability to run the company when I wasn't around. I thought more and more about selling off part of the company to investors. If that kind of a move gave me more time to be with my family and ride my cycle, then maybe it wasn't such a bad thing.

A journal entry best describes the last night of our travels:

> The last night on our trip we stayed at LaVale, Maryland—
> the town I named LaVale after eighteen years ago, almost to
> the day. It was nice to see the town, but I had so many memo-
> ries flooding my mind. I had a rough night and I wonder why
> memories can be so powerful and affect me so negatively.

In any case, Jonas and I arrived home feeling refreshed and ready to move forward. LaVale lived with us at the house, and I enjoyed her company. I tried to fix good meals for her, and we often found ourselves talking over coffee. Our relationship grew closer, but I still held my breath, waiting for the next argument to smash our fragile peace.

I walked out of one of our management team meetings we held in the boardroom and returned to my office just down the hall. Yet another management team meeting from which I left feeling confused, frustrated, and somewhat discouraged. On one hand, the business continued to grow in amazing ways. By the beginning of 1994, we had opened 279 stores with another twenty to thirty locations in the pipeline and sold over thirty million pretzels. Our franchisees seemed happy, the employees motivated, and Auntie Anne's Soft Pretzels turned up in all of the major business publications as one of the best-run franchises in the country.

On the other hand, Auntie Anne's was now made up of both family and non-family members, pressed for faster growth, and responding to a growing demand for locations. In 1994 we received more than ten requests per day from people wanting more information on opening an Auntie Anne's, yet our resources could barely stretch in order to open fifty stores in a year. And because we grew so fast over such a large area, a need arose for franchise support at a regional level, which meant opening four or five regional offices. Finally, there were shopping malls desperate to open an Auntie Anne's in areas where we did not currently have franchisees—if we wanted to open in those locations, we would have to open them as company-owned stores, something for which we did not have the cash.

We had only recently borrowed about $1.5 million, and the banks wouldn't come through for any additional money. I began to feel very controlled by our growing business. It no longer felt like the company Jonas and I started simply to bless people—it felt very corporate, very professional (in a negative way), and began to lose some of its special qualities, at least in my eyes. Now, I know there was no other way—whenever a company grows as quickly as ours did, becoming corporate is an inevitable part of the process.

My suggestion to build "one . . . store . . . at . . . a . . . time," wasn't realistic, was too shortsighted, or didn't make sense for a growing company such as ours. We all wanted to have a nationwide presence, and even international opportunities began presenting themselves. Finally I agreed that we should begin looking into other ways of raising the money.

Carl and I met a lot in those days, talking all the time. He began talking to me about another way we might be able to raise the money we needed: venture capital. Now, I knew nothing about venture capital and barely understood terms like *investor* and *equity* or *shareholders*. Carl tried to explain to me how the money would help us grow the company to a certain size, and that when we reached that size the venture capitalists would own a certain amount of the company while I owned another amount. I still didn't find the whole situation very easy to understand, but I thought it sounded like a viable idea.

During those years many different people approached me with an interest in buying a portion of the company. Some were good people whom I'd known for a long time and trusted, even a few family members; others were complete strangers or representatives from other companies. But my main concern when even considering these options always came back to my desire to give in a huge way.

In those days our giving completely funded Jonas's Family Resource and Counseling Center because we provided all of the counseling free of charge for anyone who came. I thought it would be nearly impossible to bring in other owners who felt as strongly as I did about giving. When we gave, we tried to be fiscally responsible and use the applicable tax breaks, but tax breaks have never been the main reason for my giving, and if I felt called to give to a certain cause and found out it wasn't tax deductible, I still gave. But if we sold a portion of the company to someone without the same philosophy, then what? What would happen when someone else owned the company, too, and could veto my desire to give to this individual, this charity, or that organization? That was my greatest fear.

I finally agreed to go ahead with the venture capitalist idea and asked Carl to organize a deal for the funds we needed to expand.

"All I want is one thing," I said. If we get to the very end of the deal and I'm not comfortable with it, then we walk away. I don't know enough about this kind of thing to commit one hundred percent, so as long as I can say no at the end if I want to, then we can go for it."

Carl agreed, and soon we found ourselves driving back and forth to New York City meeting with brokers and potential investors. I began praying earnestly and told God that I would not go ahead unless I got an obvious green light, a sign that venture capital was the way we should go.

❖

The night before my first television appearance, I was extremely nervous. I couldn't believe I was about to go on television and talk about my horrible past, the things I was so ashamed of, and the things that brought me so much sadness. But at some level I realized that my purpose in life might be to share my story in order to give others hope. Back in 1994 this realization just began taking hold of me, but I didn't live it out. I wanted to live my life in total transparency, always revealing the truth and not hiding issues. This appearance was the beginning of a long road to the transparent life I live today.

When I got on air, I felt a calm descend on me, and things flowed very well. The host treated me with great respect and kindness. She asked about the death of Angie, my experience with Pastor, and my relationship with Jonas. We talked about how all of these things brought about Auntie Anne's Soft Pretzels as well as Jonas's counseling organization, the Family Resource and Counseling Center.

At the end of it, contrary to the embarrassment I thought I would experience, I actually felt relieved that my story was out there! In some ways it was a confessional to my family as well, an official time to talk to them about it—I had more than twenty-five friends and family members in the audience, and I felt their support before, during, and after the taping. Before going on air, I spoke with our company's marketing manager about the interview, and he strongly discouraged me from talking about my past. Something inside of me, however, knew the time had come to put my secret out in the open, and that televised interview became a moment of truth for me, a turning point in my life.

❖

Another experience in 1994 led to my determination to confess my past and my feelings more openly, and it started under rather depressing circumstances: spending Thanksgiving on my own in Florida. Jonas had traveled to Buffalo to celebrate with the girls (my daughter LaWonna opened two Auntie Anne's stores in

New York, so LaVale moved in with her and helped run the business). I had some pressing things to attend to in Boynton Beach, Florida, and stayed in a condo owned by our friends.

While I was there, I spent a lot of time thinking about where the business was financially and wondering how we would come up with the additional needed funds. While I missed spending the holidays with my family, Florida in November can be a wonderful place: the temperature usually hovers around perfect, the evenings seem longer and more relaxing, and there's nothing like enjoying a meal with a view of the ocean. The turning point of the trip came over one of these meals—I met up with a friend who just happened to be a therapist.

At one point during our time together, we began talking about my past and how I had dealt (or hadn't dealt) with my life's experiences. She is a kind woman, very intelligent, and at the time was a practicing psychologist.

"I am amazed you have made it this far without any sort of therapy," she commented while we sat across from each other enjoying dinner.

"Really?" I said. "I've never really thought about counseling."

"I would highly recommend you commit to one year of therapy," she said. "I think there are probably a lot of issues that you still need to work through."

For the next few days, I thought about her suggestion. Just the thought of going into therapy for an entire year sounded like a completely impossible proposition, and maybe even a waste of time. But talking to her, just for those few days we were together, started a healing process in me that I could tell would not continue unless I worked at it. I began to realize that after my experience with Pastor, I had huge issues with anyone I perceived as trying to control me—something that explained my reaction to my daughters, my husband, even work colleagues (including my brothers and sisters). I arrived back in Pennsylvania determined to focus on healing and restoration for my inner self.

Meanwhile, our quest for financing continued. When we first met with the broker who was going to work with us to find investors, I was very up front about our company's mission to give, as well as the overall importance of financially supporting Jonas's counseling center, and at first we weren't sure if that could be honored in this kind of a venture. But eventually the firm representative came back to us and said, "You know, we have met with a lot of companies, but we have never met with a company like Auntie Anne's where their sole mission is to give as much as possible. But we feel we have come up with a plan. We respect your desire to give and we appreciate that, so this is the plan."

I trusted the information they presented me with, and I trusted Carl, so eventually I agreed to continue moving forward with the plan. As time went on, I became more and more serious about using venture capital. We continued meeting with a firm on a regular basis and seemed to be making progress in spite of the fact that the $3 million we required is a rather small amount when it comes to venture capitalists who are more accustomed to investing tens or hundreds of millions in a young company. Then one day while driving in my car, I suddenly felt as if God was speaking to me. Once again, not in an audible voice but just in my mind, giving me wisdom.

I found myself telling God, "I still don't see a green light about this. *I have to know*, is this the right thing for us to do as a company? Is this the way you want me to go? I need a green light—I have to see an obvious sign."

Suddenly in my mind I felt God saying, "It will be made *very* clear to you."

That promise came to me two months before we were scheduled to sign the final papers. How could I have known that God needed me to go through this process in order to learn some very important lessons, both in business and about myself?

❖

The night before our final meeting, at which I was supposed to sign the final papers with the venture capitalists, I flew in from the Houston ICSC and arrived home after midnight, and still the light looked yellow. I had not received the green light from God that I was waiting for. Jonas and I were in bed, and I was reading, but I put the book down because I couldn't hold it in any longer.

"Jonas," I said, not sure if I was going to get mad or start crying, "I am supposed to sign these papers tomorrow giving away a portion of our company to these VCs, but God has been completely silent. I haven't gotten a red or a green light yet! And he told me, very specifically that day while I was driving in the car, that he would give me a green light if I was supposed to go forward. I haven't gotten anything, Jonas. Nothing! What am I supposed to do? It's not clear to me, and tomorrow they are coming for my signature!"

I was on the verge of panic. But Jonas just looked at me with a confused look on his face, remained completely calm, and told me exactly what I needed to hear.

"Honey, it's not tomorrow morning yet."

But Jonas's words, as wise as they were, didn't comfort me. I thought to myself that maybe I had missed the green light, and I began going back over all of the events leading up to that day. Did God speak to me in circumstances I didn't fully understand? Could the green light have been the fact that we got so far, that we actually found someone willing to give us the money in spite of my refusal to budge on giving? *Not good enough*, I thought to myself. He had told me it would be a clear yes or no. I fell asleep.

❖

The next morning my stomach felt jittery as I prepared to go into the office. Finally they arrived, five or six men in very expensive suits looking out of place in our rather simple office building tucked away in the hills. The brokers were there with the gentlemen from the venture capital firm in New York, three or four of whom I'd never met before. I was the only woman. Eventually we made our way into the boardroom and talked the polite talk of businesspeople.

All the time I kept thinking, *Why am I doing this? I don't have a green light. I cannot sign those papers without a green light.* But I was also thinking about how these businessmen had come all the way from New York. How could I disappoint them by not signing the papers? I just went through the motions, feeling completely dazed.

One of the new guys spoke up. It was time to get down to business.

"Well, it's really nice to meet you, Anne, and obviously you've built a very successful business. We are tremendously excited about the opportunity of getting involved with your company.

"First we would like to clarify our position on going public: if you do not feel prepared to take the company public within the first few years of receiving our investment, we are not sure this is a deal that we would be interested in finalizing."

My stomach dropped. I didn't know how I felt about going public, and didn't know enough about the process to have a firm opinion either way, but I knew I didn't like how it sounded. But that wasn't the end of it.

"Before we go on any further," he continued, "I must admit there is one question that has been nagging me for quite some time, something I have to ask you."

"Sure, go ahead," I said, my stomach feeling rather sick.

He leaned forward, his elbows on the table, looked me square in the eyes, and asked me the question.

"I am just puzzled. Why do you think you have to give away such astronomical amounts of money?"

The blood drained from my face, and I could feel the room beginning to spin, but I returned his gaze.

"I am very disappointed that you would bring that up at this point in our negotiations," I said, "because I felt I was very clear with your people up front that, although you don't understand this, and I don't expect you to understand it, we are a company created to give. I know you have made provisions for that in the agreement, but I am very disappointed that you have to ask that question, at this time, because I thought that was answered at the very beginning of our negotiations."

"Oh no," he said quickly, "we applaud that; we respect that. I just needed to ask you the question. I was just curious on a more personal level."

The meeting continued, but I didn't think I could go on. I began feeling like I was about to have a panic attack, feeling as though I had to get out of that room at any cost. I was feeling hot and finding it difficult to breathe. About fifteen minutes after he asked the question, I excused myself and made my way to the bathroom. At that point I wasn't even thinking about the red or green light; I simply thought about the fact that if I didn't get out of that room, I was going to make a fool of myself.

As I walked out of the room, one of the brokers, Tom, followed me—he had been such a huge encouragement throughout the entire capitalization process. He, along with his firm, stood to make thousands of dollars if everything went through, just for bringing the deal together.

"Anne," he said, putting his hand on my shoulder, "you are not comfortable with this, are you?"

"No, I'm not," I said, feeling embarrassed. "Do you think anyone else noticed?"

"No, but I feel I know you pretty well, and I can tell you weren't happy with his comments on going public and your decision to give so much."

"Tom, I can't do this."

"Well," he said confidently, "then we won't."

"You mean we can just say the deal is off?"

"We'll go through the rest of the process here today. Then Jim and I will meet with you and Jonas tomorrow morning at a restaurant for coffee. Does that sound okay?"

"Okay," I said, and eventually I went back into the meeting room for the rest of the three- or four-hour meeting. I felt much better since Tom had assured me I didn't have to sign on the dotted line that day.

Finally, at the end of the meeting, Tom thanked everyone for coming and said to the gentlemen, "Just give us a couple more days to talk things over, and we'll be in touch."

After the meeting, I felt embarrassed that they had come all the way from New York when I didn't even think we were going to do the deal. I also felt bad for Carl and the team and dreaded telling them my decision, or what I thought my decision was going to be. The management team would have benefitted financially if the deal went through. I couldn't take the pressure, so I just left and went home.

The next morning Jonas and I met with the brokers of our venture capitalist deal, Tom and Jim. It was early, and the sound of stirring spoons against the insides of coffee cups seemed the loudest sound. Tom eventually broached the subject, jumping right into the topic I wanted to talk about.

"Jonas and Anne, Jim and I have talked at length about your situation, this deal that's lined up."

Then he said something that made my eyes open wide as saucers.

". . . And we don't think you should do it."

A weight lifted off of me in an instant, and I simply can't explain it. That was the signal I had been waiting for, and it was most definitely red. What kind of signal could it be, when two men who stood to gain so much if the deal went through just sat there and told me they didn't think I should do it? Energy pulsed through my body—I could have run a marathon, I felt so revitalized.

"God told me he would give me a clear signal," I told those

two brokers with tears in my eyes. "Thank you for your willingness to give me the answer."

"This is not normal for us to do," Tom said. "We're not in the business of passing up on deals. But I know you well enough to know you are not comfortable, that you're unsure about giving up ownership in your company, and I want to support you."

We sat and talked for a while, and I felt like a new person. But as we stood up to go, the reality of the situation confronted me, and I turned to Tom again.

"Tom, what am I going to tell the management team?"

"They're not going to be happy," he said in a serious voice. "They've put a lot of time and effort into this project. They won't like your decision."

For a while I just sat at my desk, trying to gather the courage I needed to make my announcement. Then I went into Carl's office and told him.

"I decided not to do the deal with the VCs. Please let the management team know," I said.

That was it. I stood there for a few moments before walking out. That was all I said—if I said any more, I knew I would cry.

There are many difficult things about working with family, and of all the family members I worked with, *I* was probably the most difficult! Fortunately, through all of the trials and arguments and disagreements, all eight of us still remain great friends to this day and spend a lot of time together.

I will write more about working with family in a later chapter, but at that time in 1995, things became more difficult for me personally. It was time for some of my darkest secrets to be revealed.

Anne (2nd from left) with her brothers and sister

Anne, age 16

Jonas and Anne's engagement picture

Auntie Anne in front of the first store in Downingtown, Pennsylvania

Anne and her mother, Amanda Smucker

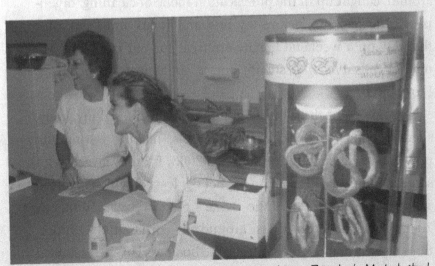

Auntie Anne and daughter LaWonna at the Harrisburg, Pennsylvania Market stand

CHAPTER TEN

No More Secrets

When the secret is told, the stronghold is broken.

—Dr. Richard Dobbins

That day in 2003 seemed nearly perfect. I felt myself bustling around, caught up in the pre-vacation mode of cleaning, organizing, and packing, before my husband Jonas and I left later that day on a weekend business retreat for our company. My mother calls it *butzing*, staying busy at an almost frenzied pace. I love butzing.

At some point the whirlwind that was me entered my study, slicing open envelopes, reading e-mails, making last-minute phone calls. During the summer of 2003, I found myself with some major decisions coming up, not the least of which involved selling the company, Auntie Anne's Soft Pretzels. With our 700th domestic location just around the corner, and 119 locations in twelve foreign countries, the business barely resembled the small farmers' market stand Jonas and I started in 1988. I also hoped to finish my first shot at a book, just something simple geared toward children, with beautiful illustrations and warm images from my childhood. Auntie Anne's Soft Pretzels served as my life for the fifteen years leading up to 2003, but things seemed to be shifting. A restlessness crept into my spirit—I felt the time to move on coming just around the corner.

Even more important, though, for the first time in my life I felt completely whole. The depression I experienced off and on throughout my life began dissolving, my family recovered from many hard knocks, and I no longer depended on the affirmation of others to build up my self-esteem. I could handle conflict without breaking down. Life felt good.

Then the phone rang.

"Hello?"

"Anne?" It was my personal assistant. "I've got an e-mail I need to show you, and you're not going to like this."

She told me who sent the e-mail, and immediately I knew the content. I asked her to please bring the e-mail to the house—I didn't trust the privacy of the Internet enough for her to forward it to me. We didn't speak long, and she made the drive from our corporate office to my house in less than ten minutes.

I watched for her car from my office window, wanting to catch her before she rang the bell or knocked on the door—I didn't want Jonas to know she was there. He might, just in passing, ask why she stopped by the house. I would tell him, of course, but not until I could think it through, prepare myself. I paced back and forth, my stomach knotted, and when she turned into our lane, I walked outside to meet her. She handed the sheet of paper to me.

"We received this e-mail." She knew the potential harm it could do to the business, to my reputation. "It was directed to the Web site. We'll try to contain it. No one else has seen it."

I retreated to my office, up the stairs, past the photos of our daughters, our grandchildren, the family picture of me with my five brothers and two sisters. Going up those steps felt like climbing a mountain. Finally in my office, I read the e-mail through tears of frustration: "Everyone thinks Auntie Anne is so perfect . . . well I know something about Anne that you don't know . . . When everyone thought she was away . . . traveling around the world . . . affair . . ."

I cried, trying to figure out how I would ever tell Jonas about the secret I'd kept for eight years. Our marriage had survived the loss of his brother in a motorcycle accident, the loss of our daughter, the abuse of power and position by our pastor, the growth of a business: would this cost me everything? At that point I realized I could not let myself be surprised if Jonas left me. I had to prepare for the worst.

My mind couldn't help but drift back. Just the thought of those years, from the end of 1994 up through 1996, made me shudder. That was when LaWonna told us about what happened to her as a child. I entered into major depression. Nearly lost the company. Nearly walked away from everything.

I closed my eyes. And while the anger and helplessness and sadness did not by any means vanish, I could feel something like relief welling up to fill in empty spaces. Finally this secret could no longer keep me prisoner. The truth would come out.

On a cold day in February 1995, the twenty-second to be exact, my daughter LaWonna and I drove to see my therapist. None of my family ever went along to my counseling sessions, but on that particular morning LaWonna asked me if she could accompany me and tell me something at the session.

"You can tell me now, if you want."

"That's okay, Mom. I'd rather wait until we're there."

Hmmm, I thought. *Okay.* Well, I always asked my daughters if they wanted to join me for counseling, so perhaps this answered my prayers. I always thought open communication and talking about our problems would help. We put on our coats and left the house.

My curiosity got the better of me, so in the car I asked her again.

"So, LaWonna, what's this about?"

"Oh, I'll tell you about that when we get there."

"I know. I just thought maybe . . ."

LaWonna interrupted.

"No," she said, smiling but firm, "I'll tell you about it when we get there." When she said those words, she reminded me so much of when she was just a little girl, keeping secrets.

We arrived at the rustic house that included the office. On the way inside, I couldn't stop wondering what LaWonna would tell me. *Did she have an abortion when she was younger? Please, no.* I thought that would devastate me. Then I thought, *No, she's going to tell me something about drugs.* Nothing I came up with in my mind could have prepared me.

We got into the office, and LaWonna and I sat across the desk from my therapist. She is a kind counselor with brown hair and brown eyes. For a few moments small talk and polite smiles made their way around the room. Then she turned to LaWonna.

"Well, LaWonna, I know that when you called me, you said there was something you'd like to tell your mother. Are you ready to tell her?"

"Yes."

My twenty-three year-old LaWonna looked me right in the eye. While so much about her had changed in the previous twenty-three years, she still looked at me through those beautiful brown eyes.

"Mom, he did it to me too." Her lip quivered.

Silence. Maybe I knew exactly what she meant the instant she said it, but my mind wouldn't allow the information to process immediately. Maybe total disgust blocked my mind from traveling that road myself.

"What?"

Silence, only a second, and then it registered.

I cursed, perhaps the first obscenity I ever spoke in front of anyone. From deep down inside of me, I felt evil erupting like a volcano, and I felt victimized once again. All of my old wounds ripped open.

"LaWonna!" I yelled. "Why didn't you tell me before?" As soon as the words entered the room, I knew they were all wrong. They hung in the air like a foul odor. I didn't want to accuse her. I wanted to keep her safe. I wanted to go back in time and protect her, be a better mother, the kind of mother who kept closer watch over her children and didn't let those things happen. But I couldn't do that. I felt utterly helpless, defeated. I felt as if I were being haunted with my past, and it felt worse than my own abuse.

Something clicked in my brain. When Angie died, we mourned her death with friends and family, the people from our church showing tremendous support. But my daughter LaWonna died, too, years ago, and no one knew. Her spirit killed by the perpetrator—no one brought flowers, no one mourned.

That day came and went, one of the worst days of my life.

During the coming months, nights would slow to a standstill. I spent a lot of time wandering the house in search of peace long after everyone else fell asleep. Even when sleep finally came, it rarely took me from those troubles, only down into the frightening depths of nightmares I couldn't figure out.

In my dream LaWonna was six months old and I felt myself being forced to bury her alive. She wasn't dead, but someone or something forced me to put her in a casket and bury her! "I can't do this, I can't do this," I sobbed. Then suddenly, in a flash, she grew older, nine or ten years old, and again I felt forced to bury her. "I can't do this, I can't do this."

I woke up sweating, crying.

As 1995 progressed, I began to withdraw from my family, my friends. The business provided the perfect cover, giving me ample opportunities to travel unaccompanied, away from my house, which was saturated with chaos and conflict. I just wanted alone time, lots of it. Plus, the business made me look like a success—by the summer of 1995, we approached our 300th location and prepared for international expansion. I enjoyed the accolades I received while circulating in the business world and by choice became more and more immersed in it, drawn farther away from a home life filled with pain.

Then the deal became final: we would open our first international store in Indonesia! We never planned to expand overseas, but an Indonesian businessman persisted. Pretzels would work, he said. The product tastes too good not to work. After years and years of our turning him down because we never felt ready, he finally convinced us to give him the green light. Excitement filled the air at our corporate office. International expansion served as yet another confirmation of our success, my success, and it opened up so much potential for growth in the future. I began preparations to leave for the Far East in order to arrive in time for the grand opening of Auntie Anne's international store number one. Privately, the thought of being alone for two weeks, literally as far away from Lancaster as I could get, filled me with a huge sense of relief.

There was something fateful about our first international location sprouting up in Indonesia. An Indonesian missionary to the United States had led me to a more Spirit-filled life way back in 1974. And now, over twenty years later, I returned to her country with *pretiolas,* little gifts. I smiled to myself.

Yet the smiles came few and far between, and the days leading up to my departure felt riddled with difficulty. First my daughter LaWonna, who had gotten married in 1993, let us know she'd decided to get a divorce. Then my unmarried nineteen-year-old daughter, LaVale, told us she was pregnant. My girls struggled, and I didn't know what I could do to change the abysmal course on which all of our lives traveled.

Not only did my two daughters struggle: I found myself in a morally compromising position with a friend. We seemed closer than we should be somehow, occasionally meeting over dinner or talking on the phone. I liked the closeness, the feeling of having him to talk to. But I didn't like how it felt at home. I didn't like the secrecy, the excuses, the lies, but this once-innocent friendship slipped down a dark road that soon led me into an affair.

On the afternoon of July 4, 1995, just before I left for the airport, Jonas, LaWonna, LaVale, and I stood in the kitchen, crying together: LaWonna with her impending breakup, LaVale under the stress of being an expectant mother, Jonas probably wondering how things had gone so wrong, and me loaded down with guilt that I was sharing my problems with another man. The girls were moving to California on July 9 to stay with family friends—LaWonna needed to get away, and LaVale wanted to go with her. They would be gone when I returned from overseas, my world disintegrating around me. What did I have to come back to? The girls would be on the other side of the country, and my relationship with Jonas was decaying. The future held only sadness and more depression.

Somehow I ended up on the 747 in Philadelphia bound for Jakarta, Indonesia, with two layovers on the way. I couldn't wait to leave my troubles on the ground. Unfortunately, leaving the ground didn't prove an easy task. I sat in my business-class seat, comfortable, my eyes closed, trying to escape the world. A quick escape did not exist. We sat in the plane on the tarmac for five hours.

Eventually the plane took off, but the long delay meant I missed my connection in California and was forced to spend the night. A close friend of mine, Karen Whitley, lived in California and came up to see me at the hotel. I think I stayed in a Marriott. We went out to eat, and I couldn't stop crying, spilling my guts about my family, my girls, the problems Jonas and I were experiencing, everything except the affair.

"You shouldn't be traveling by yourself," she whispered. I could tell she felt scared for me.

"I'll be fine. I'll be fine," I kept repeating.

I boarded the plane in California, this time the destination Tai Pei, but was only confronted with another delay, four more hours, also on the tarmac, this time due to poor visibility. By now I felt exhausted, drained from crying all night and weighed down by the worries I couldn't stop thinking about. Finally the plane took off. The sixteen-hour flight from California to Tai Pei became an endless stream of tears, trips to the bathroom, anything but the sleep I so desperately needed. Even in the sky, thousands of miles from home, I could not find peace.

Because of the delay in California, I missed my flight in Tai Pei. I felt very vulnerable there, surrounded by a foreign language, a foreign culture. The color gray dominated the airport, everything so drab and unfeeling. After finally finding someone who could speak English, I prepared for the last leg of my journey, a four-hour flight. Finally I arrived in Indonesia, and the Auntie Anne's licensees met me at the airport, placed me and my luggage in their Mercedes, and whisked me off in the direction of my hotel.

Business mode kicked in. My knack for compartmentalizing took over. Suddenly, on the outside, I acted vibrant and excited, ready for our first international opening. I became interested in other people's lives, became passionate about the product and the business, became the person who made Auntie Anne's so successful. I couldn't wait to see their location and their country. I probably seemed ready to take the soft pretzel message around the world. But on the inside I crept lower and lower.

On the way to the hotel, I saw things I'd never seen before. Intense poverty across the street from the most glamorous hotels in the world. Masses of people and mopeds and cars turned a four-lane highway into an eight-lane parking lot. For nearly an hour we sat there, completely stationary in a traffic jam. I ran out of things to talk about, started to feel claustrophobic. Then we moved an inch. And another inch. Then we moved faster. Finally we saw the problem: in the middle of the highway, a donkey slowly pulled a wagon down the road. I realized I was not in America anymore.

Our driver turned down back alleys and side streets to avoid the traffic. Poverty cried out from every turn. Small shanty houses piled up against each other, overlooking the river littered with floating debris. Barefoot children covered in sludge played in the streets, dodging cars and motorcycles and horse-drawn wagons. "Lord, why have you brought me here?" I asked.

We arrived at the hotel sixty-one hours after I walked out the front door of my house in Pennsylvania. I couldn't have felt any farther from home.

❖

The next day I met up with a few colleagues from Auntie Anne's who traveled to Indonesia before me to help with the training and setup of the first store. The licensees took us on a tour of the city, and we visited a few potential locations. Staying busy kept my mind off my troubles, at least for a few hours at a time. But I felt exhausted from the journey, having never crossed so many time zones, and the constant transition from scenes of affluence to scenes of poverty began wearing on me, increasing my depression. How could it be fair that God blessed me with so much yet seemed to leave these people in their misery? Besides increasing my sadness, though, the sights of cardboard houses and young children going to the bathroom in the river opened my eyes to the needs in the world. In the years to come, we would begin exploring how to channel some of Auntie Anne's resources into helping people like the ones I saw in Indonesia.

That evening the licensees took us out for dinner, a wonderful meal but foreign to my body's normal intake of meat and potatoes. I retreated to my suite high up in a magnificent hotel in Jakarta. The pillows sat fluffed; the linens smelled fresh. I sat by the telephone and cried, feeling so safe in that room yet so cheerless. I wanted to go out and walk the streets. In my depression I felt no fear for any harm that might come to me. I think that perhaps I wished something bad would happen, something that would give me the excuse to flee this life of grief. I called one of my Auntie Anne's colleagues who was also in the country for this opening. A good friend of mine. Someone I could trust. I couldn't tell this person about all of my problems, not the affair, but at least I would have someone to talk to.

"I'm feeling horrible. I can't stop crying."

"Can I come over?" the voice said on the other line. "Should we go out for a cup of coffee?"

Soon I met my friend (and employee) in the hotel lobby, and the two of us left in a cab for someplace close, somewhere I could talk.

"I just want to get drunk," I said, still crying. I never drank, not even a drop of alcohol, and Auntie Anne's company-wide ban on drinking during work trips was absolute.

"You don't want to do that."

"Oh yes, I do," I said, half laughing and half crying. "I do. I just want to get away. I can't handle life anymore."

"Well, I don't think you want to get drunk. But if you do, I'll be here and won't let anything bad happen to you."

I had too much to drink, and my good friend helped me to my hotel, leaving me there alone. What unbelievable shame I felt when I woke up the next morning! Even now this story is one of the most embarrassing for me to tell. There I was, someone who sat on Christian boards of directors, someone people looked up to for inspiration, consuming too much alcohol on a business trip, not to mention doing it in front of an employee!

Today it's hard for me to believe I could feel that hopeless, that I actually believed by simply drinking enough I could escape the pain. I guess the main reason I'm so disappointed in how I behaved is that I strongly believe leaders in any organization should serve as good examples and be people of integrity. During that night in Indonesia, I sank to an all-time low. I didn't live up to my own high standards, and my failure that night filled me with even more guilt, continuing the downward spiral.

The next day's grand opening of Auntie Anne's provided me with a much-needed burst of positive feelings. The store buzzed, the pretzels baked to perfection and shaped just right, the many employees sampling and giving perfect customer service: I looked at the pretzels and said, "Wow! Yes! This is what Auntie Anne's is all about!" I felt so thankful for great licensees who were willing to take the risk of selling a brand-new product, pretzels, one that didn't even have a name in their own language.

I stood there looking at the balloons, the banners, the shop, the sampling taking place, the lines beginning to form. I couldn't believe how far we'd come in only seven years. Within the next six months, we would open stores in the Philippines as well, with many more countries around the world beginning to express interest in selling our soft pretzels.

Back in my hotel, packing my suitcase, I felt overwhelmed with two completely different trains of thought, the first being amazement that God trusted me with this business. In spite of the horrible things I'd done in my life, the poor decisions I was making even at that time, the business continued to grow: opening an international location reminded me that the sky was the limit. If I, an ex-Amish girl, could somehow manage to lead a company through this kind of growth, anything could happen. But despair still overwhelmed me. I did not want to go home. I did not want to go back to the office. I simply wanted to run away somewhere, leave the business and the success that both inspired and suffocated me, leave my family with all of their issues, leave my husband with whom I could no longer communicate. But where? There was nowhere else for me to go. So I boarded the 747 and began the long journey back to a place that never felt less like home.

After hours and hours of flight, the plane approached Philadelphia. I found myself writing faster than I knew I could, page after scribbled page addressed to God confessing my anger, my disappointment, my hurt, my depression. As the plane descended, my insides erupted onto the page. I told God exactly how I felt. I sensed an interruption in my thoughts, a persistent thought louder than my own that said, "I will make a way for you."

My heart resisted. "But, God, how will you do this for me?"

"I will make a way for you."

"But, God, I've had enough. I'm giving up. I hate my life. I'm angry at my children for being out of control. I'm angry at Jonas for not trying hard enough to understand me. I don't see any way out."

"I will make a way for you."

Leaving the plane, I held those sheets of paper tightly in my fist. I threw them into the first trash can I found, unable to bear the thought of the severe humiliation I would feel if anyone read them, if anyone had any idea to what depths I sank during those times. But for the first time in over a year, I felt the slightest breath of hope. He would make a way. I walked down the concourse, my baggage not quite so heavy.

❖

The leaves changed color, and the holidays were just around the corner. During those autumn months of 1995, I wrote in my journal that I felt the slightest of improvements—if I measured my emotional state on a scale of 1 to 10, I went from 0 to 1. Not a huge improvement, but the beginning. A change in my daughters' circumstances may have explained why life felt lighter: they moved from California to Texas to open their own Auntie Anne's Soft Pretzels location, to our old home filled with so many good memories. It was a homecoming for them, and their house became a place for me to go, a place to escape to when the business or my disillusion with my own home life overwhelmed me. Friends also gathered around me during that year, providing much-needed support and care.

I remember meeting with one of those friends, my sister-in-law Verna. We talked over coffee. She was one of the few people I trusted enough to talk to about everything in my life. At that point I felt decision-making time pressing down. Would I leave my husband, my family, my business, everything I knew, for a new start?

"I know I'm a good girl, Verna. I know I am. I've always tried to make the right decision. But right now, I just want to walk away from everything. It's all too much. I want to be a bad girl."

Somehow Verna convinced me to stay, to make the right decision, but I still walked through limbo until another old friend called me with advice I will never forget.

Oliver, a missionary friend from Sweden, called me shortly after my discussion with Verna. He and I spoke only once every few years. At that point he knew nothing about what I had gone through during the earlier part of that year. When I heard his voice on the other end of the line, I smiled.

"Anne," he said kindly, "God wants me to tell you something."

"Oh, okay. What is it?"

"You are a good girl. God has forgiven you for everything you've done in the past, and he will forgive you for anything you do in the future."

How could he have known to say that exact phrase—"you are a good girl"? I had only whispered that to my very close friend Vern.

The tide in my life, pulling me into the abyss, began to turn.

❖

Time passed, and still I waited for God to make a way for me. On August 12, 1996, Jonas and I got on our bikes at 4:00 in the afternoon after a difficult day at the office. My brother Carl and I had waded through some tough topics, things requiring resolution. I never enjoyed those types of discussions and usually ended up responding in one of two ways: either the other person tried to control me and I became confrontational, or I lost my nerve, breaking down in tears of anxiety. Back then I was a wounded soldier, but I hid it well. How could I expect anyone else to know how fragile I felt?

When four o'clock arrived, I almost laughed out loud with relief: gliding out our driveway into a beautiful August day, heading toward my favorite kind of vacation, full of long days on my motorcycle rolling down gorgeous roads. I still felt down. I still struggled to take the right road. But in the back of my head, I began to hear a voice telling me the same thing I heard on the plane during my trip home from Indonesia.

"I will make a way for you."

I cried a lot on our trip, sometimes communicating to Jonas my need to pull over. He saw the tears, realized something was wrong, and as our trip turned back to the north, he began to encourage me.

"Anne, why don't we just stop and see Doc? I'm sure he could help you."

Doc was Dr. Dobbins, a counselor and founder of EMERGE Ministries. I'd attended a counseling session with him a year or two earlier but revealed very little about my true self.

"Well, Anne," he said to me in a kind voice after that first and only session. "I think you're handling things just fine. I think you're doing okay." How I treasured those words and used them to rationalize my behavior! *Doc says I'm okay,* I said to myself, *so I must be okay.* But his diagnosis was based solely on faulty information. Later Doc told me he knew I'd hidden most of the truth about myself from him, but there seemed little he could do until I became willing to share my heart.

"I know Doc could help you. Why don't we just swing by Akron and see him?"

Finally Jonas called, and Doc's wife, Priscilla, answered. She would love to meet us for breakfast. Doc couldn't make it, but she would be there. God was making a way for me.

Tears came again at breakfast with Priscilla.

"I just don't know what's wrong with me," I said to Priscilla.

"Oh, Anne, just set up a time to talk with Doc. He can help you. I know he can."

I didn't want to talk to Doc. I knew he could get the truth out of me, and fear welled up inside of me at the thought of the truth coming out. The truth about Auntie Anne, about how I felt, about my mental state.

"Anne, just call him," Priscilla pleaded.

Finally, amid my protests, she dialed the number and held the phone up to my ear. I kept shaking my head—no—I didn't want to talk. Doc answered.

"Hello?"

"Doc, it's me, Anne Beiler."

I couldn't stop crying.

"Doc, something's wrong with me. I don't know what to do. I can't stop crying. I cry all the time!"

Eventually, in spite of my strong hesitations and unwilling-ness, I agreed to meet Doc for a few sessions later in the month. God was making a way—I never would have called Doc had it not been for Priscilla dialing the number and hold-ing the phone up to my ear. My healing began when I dis-cussed my issues with him, including my past, my children, my marriage. I didn't walk into his office one day a shattered life and leave that afternoon completely repaired; yet some-thing about the counseling I received there started the process, piece by jagged piece.

Only one problem remained: the secret I'd confessed to God and walked away from remained unspoken.

I walked to Jonas's office, visibly shaken, the one flimsy piece of white computer paper quivering in my hand.

"Anne, what's wrong?" Jonas asked.

"Honey, I need to read you something."

After I read the e-mail, I didn't look up at him, just waited for a moment in that charged silence before speaking in a whisper: "It's true. I had an affair."

Jonas didn't say anything at first. I looked at the floor, probably the reason I can't remember the expression on his face. Of all the things he could have said, of all the accusations he could have made, the words he actually said were those I least expected.

"We have to go see Doc."

Before we left, Jonas and I drove to our corporate office to meet with Sam Beiler. By this time he had taken over running the day-to-day operations of the company. We explained the situation to him, and he told us to do whatever we needed to do, that his number one priority would be keeping the issue private and contained. I felt extremely thankful for his understanding. While I spoke with Sam, Jonas made a few quick calls and arranged a time for us to meet with Doc that weekend, the next day in fact, so we went back to the house to finish our packing, not for a weekend of business, but for what I hoped would be a weekend that could somehow save our marriage.

LaWonna was visiting us that week, and as we left the house, she could tell something wasn't right. She asked a few questions, and finally Jonas just said, "We're going to see Doc and Priscilla."

LaWonna stopped for a moment.

"What did Mom do this time?"

I have to smile now when I think back to that question.

✦

"You know, Anne," Doc said as we sat on his screened-in porch on that warm summer night, "this could be your last chance. Three strikes and you're out."

I knew he was right. I couldn't understand why Jonas still loved me after all of my mistakes. I'd hurt him deeply—I knew I had. Yet I could also feel the same slipping into the abyss that I'd felt back in 1995 when LaWonna told me about her abuse, when the company overwhelmed me, when I found myself in the middle of an affair. Feelings of shame, guilt, embarrassment, and depression tugged on my sleeve, telling me their road was my road.

"Jonas," I said, "first I have to tell you how sorry I am that I did this to you. I know God has forgiven me—I only hope that you can too. But I refuse to let myself go down the path of guilt and shame again, because that will only take me back into that black hole. I've punished myself enough. I want to move ahead, the two of us, together."

Jonas freed me from those worries. He assured me he wouldn't leave. He wanted to work with me on our relationship.

"I've felt strongly tempted to do the same thing," he told me later that night. "How can I blame you for having the affair I've nearly had many times?" He continues to amaze me.

Discussing that last secret with Jonas and Doc stirred up so many things, kind of like walking through a shallow, muddy stream. Just the thought of walking through that old stream scared me at first, but it was always there—I knew I had to cross it some day. The debris, the overturned rocks, the slimy critters dashing this way and that. But then, just when you reach the middle and everything seems as murky as it can get, the water begins carrying things downstream, washing the muck away. I crossed that river in 2003; the e-mail forced me to do that. But now I feel free from all that dirt, cleaner than ever, and ready to leave the past behind.

CHAPTER ELEVEN

A Secret Is Told

Good family life is never an accident, but always
an accomplishment by those who share it.

—JAMES H. S. BOSSARD

I had never seen our family like this.

It was a warm night in 1976, about eight months after Angie died. Outside my parents' large stone farmhouse, things probably appeared rather normal for a spring evening: the sun was setting out across the fields, the outbuildings stood calm and austere, a few of the windows were open to let the fresh spring air through. The place on the drive where Angie had died remained unmarked, as unassuming as ever. Only one thing was different and could have clued someone in to the possibility that something was wrong. Pastor sat in his car, parked in the shadows of our driveway. The snake had entered the garden.

Rumors and whispers of improper behavior spread through our church, claims that Pastor was not all he seemed to be. Our congregation, after experiencing five years of spiritual renewal, found itself caught in the midst of a tornado of suspicion and lies. Some believed the yet-unofficial charges that Pastor was acting improperly with church money and that he had been seen in questionable situations with a number of the church women. Some defended him vehemently. The church split down the middle. Our family found itself at the center of the controversy, and the fracture found its way through what was once an unbreakable family bond. Of the eight siblings, four of my brothers believed the charges that Pastor acted indecently and thought he should go; one of my brothers, my two sisters, and I refused to believe the rumors. Four versus four.

I acted in a state of denial. There were many reasons I refused to believe the rumors: first, because I was involved with him, and in spite of the nature of our first encounter, I couldn't imagine that he would be with anyone but me! Second, if I took the side of those charging Pastor, I was sure my own guilt would be exposed. I was trapped in a tangled web of silence, and only my own confession could have freed me, but I wasn't prepared to come clean, and that fact forced me to side with someone who deep down I knew was probably guilty of all charges. By staying with him and keeping quiet about what happened, I allowed him to steal my voice. Meanwhile, Pastor kept control of my two sisters and one brother by convincing them in one-on-one meetings that he was innocent.

Eventually we decided to call a family meeting.

"It can't be true! They are all just rumors," four of us maintained.

"But look at the people who are saying these things!" my brothers argued back. "These people are our friends—they wouldn't lie about something like this!"

"But this is Pastor. Why would he lie?" we replied.

And so the night went, back and forth, back and forth. The tension grew to an unbearable level. Loud voices rang out followed by long periods of silence. Some of us paced the room; others stood leaning against the counters. The air in the room felt as if it would explode with the introduction of a single spark.

At one point my brother Merrill (second to youngest), seeing Pastor's car in the drive, went out to him. He crawled into the passenger's seat and slammed the door. Turning to Pastor, he pleaded, demanded, that he come in and make things right.

"Don't you see what's happening in there? Don't you see what's happening to our family? You have to come inside. You have to come clean, make it right."

But Pastor just sat there, shaking his head as if the whole thing saddened him immensely. He was such a good actor.

"Merrill," he said firmly, "there are some things you can't really deal with. Some things you can't make better. You just have to let them go. You just have to let them run their course."

One day during the summer of 2004, Sam Beiler came into my office. Sam proved himself as one of our most dedicated employees through the years, starting in Florida as a store support representative when we opened our first stores in Florida. Then we convinced him to move to Chicago as a regional director to oversee our growth in the Midwest, even though he wanted to move back home to Pennsylvania. Finally he came back to our head office as operations director, moving up through the ranks, eventually taking over as president of the company. Sam always jumped at any opportunity, seemed willing to do whatever was required, and impressed me greatly throughout the years. I was never disappointed with the way he ran my company.

"Anne, do you have a second?" he asked and, not waiting for an answer, pulled up a chair and leaned forward. I laughed. Sam always went straight to the point.

"I've been thinking," he said. "If I can make the financial side work, would you sell Auntie Anne's to me?"

In the years leading up to that moment, Jonas and I both felt the need to begin planning for the future of the company. I suddenly realized that I wasn't going to be around forever, and so many companies fail after their founder is no longer involved, so we thought it important to plan for a transition. At that point we weren't planning specifically on selling the company, just on putting together some kind of systematic handover for when I either retired or decided to step back from my involvement with Auntie Anne's.

First we explored the possibility of passing on ownership to our daughters, the type of ownership in which one or both of them would be involved hands-on in the growth and direction of the company on a daily basis. After a few months of exploring these options and trying to figure out what that would look like, it became apparent that neither of our daughters was interested in moving in that direction.

Another option we explored was passing on ownership of the company to the employees. At this point the models we looked at started to lean more and more toward our selling the company, but with my continued involvement, albeit minimal. But the more we explored this option, the more I realized I would have the same headaches without the advantages of owning the company, so that option faded.

Finally, at one stage Jonas and I began to talk about selling the business outright, just finding a buyer and walking away. The topic came about as the result of the whole process and not really as a sudden moment of inspiration or as the result of specific circumstances. During what became years of exploring what I thought the future of the company should look like, eventually the idea of selling the company surfaced, and we began pursuing that option, but still only as a possibility, not as a foregone conclusion. I still had many questions: Did I want to sell? Would the company keep my name if I sold? How would it feel to walk up to an Auntie Anne's location and not own the company? How much could we sell the company for? And I still wasn't even sure that was the road I wanted to take.

As more time passed, I began to realize that my life's purpose was leading me farther and farther away from the business—I began to feel the pressures and responsibilities of the business getting in the way of other very important things that I felt called to do, such as speaking to people about my story, being more involved in the lives of my children and grandchildren, and supporting Jonas as he continued in his counseling endeavors.

One day Jonas asked me a tough question.

"At what age can you see yourself still running Auntie Anne's?"

I thought for a moment.

"Certainly not seventy," I said, groaning inwardly at the thought of being that old and still having so much responsibility.

"What about sixty-five?" he asked.

"I don't think so," I said slowly. "I'd want to be finished by then."

"Sixty?" he asked.

"Hmmm," I said, thinking. "Maybe."

"Well," Jonas said, "it's going to have to be sixty, because if we start the process now, you will probably be sixty by the time it's all said and done." I was around fifty-five at the time of that conversation.

I hated the thought of reaching the age of sixty-five or seventy and feeling that I still provided value to the company when in fact I might not. I saw it happen so often, in nonprofit organizations or churches or other businesses: people retaining their leadership positions, thinking they were still important to the growth of the organization, when in fact their old ways of seeing things were holding the group back. I didn't want that to be me. I didn't want to outlive my usefulness at Auntie Anne's.

Jonas, Sam Beiler, and I announced to the employees that succession planning was under way, and we also began meeting with the appropriate people to try to see what sort of options were out there for us. This more serious approach to selling the business began in the summer of 2004, and I settled in for what I expected to be a long process—an assumption that could not have been further from what we were about to experience. But as had happened so many times in my life, God's timing proved to be distinctly different from the time frame I planned. In a few short months, Sam came forward, someone I hadn't even thought about, and Jonas and I found ourselves preparing for the sale of Auntie Anne's.

Yet even after we made the final decision to sell the company to Sam, things felt strange: I still hadn't told anyone else in my family about the decision to sell. Through the years my siblings formed a vital part of my decision-making process, whether it be at the one-on-one meetings we occasionally had or at our once-a-month sibling gatherings. I asked Sam, Jonas, and the counselors walking us through the process of the sale when we should tell my siblings, and their decision was unanimous: to involve everyone at this point would only muddy the waters, possibly confuse the issue. It would be best to wait until everything was finalized before making the announcement. I accepted their guidance, but something inside me felt guilty, something felt my silence was a form of betrayal to my brothers and sisters.

❖

After that family meeting in 1976, there seemed no possibility of reconciliation. The four boys and my parents, all of whom believed the rumors circulating about Pastor, became less involved in the church. My other brother, my two sisters, and I each became more and more convinced of his innocence, once again because of the one-on-one time he spent with each of us. His smooth talking and ability to maintain composure under the most implicating of circumstances convinced us. Yet Pastor wasn't content to just divide us four from four—he continued the division until the four of us on his side could barely spend time together.

Eventually the pressure on him to leave the church, as well as mounting evidence of his wrongdoing, forced him out, and in November 1976 he left Pennsylvania, moved to another state, and started a church there. Still I didn't feel free from him: we spoke on the phone, and he remained the one person I shared everything with, whether it was my increasing unhappiness in Pennsylvania or my deteriorating relationship with Jonas. I still felt trapped and controlled by Pastor. Shortly after he left, my sister Fi and her husband, Mike, also moved to that state.

I didn't think life could get any worse. Not only had our family split, our church crumbled, and my confidant fled, but now the singing group formed by my two sisters and me dissolved. We had sung together for ten years, and now that was over, too, yet another destruction brought about by Pastor. I felt an overwhelming desire to leave Lancaster County, to escape all of these horrible events, to try to find a new beginning in a faraway place. Then a job opportunity arose for Jonas and my brother-in-law Aaron in Texas—finally something to grasp onto, something to carry us through life. Becky, Aaron, Jonas, and I decided to leave these old fields and rolling hills. Too much pain surrounded us.

As I mentioned earlier, the most difficult part for me about leaving Pennsylvania was leaving Angie buried at the church. I felt I was abandoning her. As I boxed all of her little clothes and toys, I couldn't help but wonder if her death hadn't led to all of the other horrible things that had happened to me and my family. I didn't think I would ever be close to her again, and I was frightened that my memories of her would somehow fade if we left the place she had lived her short life.

So torn was our family that my parents didn't even help us pack. I don't think any of my brothers came by to help, and even though we lived right next door, Daddy didn't come to help us load the truck. Not that I blame them—I probably didn't even want to see them anymore at that point. My mom came down to say good-bye but couldn't stop crying and eventually went back to the house.

"It's just too sad," she said as she walked out the door. She spent an entire week in bed after we left, her heart completely broken. I remember thinking that the whole concept of family as I knew it up to that point in my life was over. I couldn't imagine how things could possibly heal.

Eventually we finished packing and the four of us got into

the car: Jonas, LaVale, LaWonna, and me. It was June 1977. We may have said a quick good-bye to Mom and Dad, I can't remember, but if we did, it certainly wasn't anything big. Soon we hit the road, driving the twenty-four-plus hours that separated us from a new life. I hoped it would be a better life.

I don't think we talked to any family in Pennsylvania for a couple of months after we got to Texas. Jonas settled into his new job; LaWonna started school. I think the first call we got was from Daddy. His mother, my grandmother, was deathly ill—could we come home?

"I'm sorry, Daddy, we just don't have the money," I explained quietly.

She died soon after, and we didn't go back for the funeral either. For a family who only a few short years earlier would have done anything to be together during a difficult time, this lack of response on our part can only serve to show just how bad things had become. With each such circumstance we grew further and further apart.

Then another call a few months later.

"Your mother has taken ill," Daddy said quietly over the phone. "She can't get out of bed. She's not doing well."

Still we stayed away. Eventually Mom recovered, but I can't think back on those years without a heavy heart regarding the way we treated my parents, the disregard and almost contempt with which we handled those family situations. And all because we allowed a pastor to come into our family, take us into his confidence, and then pit us one against the other.

My sister Fi and her husband, Mike, decided to join us in Texas, and then came the news that filled me with such strange emotions: word reached Jonas and me that Pastor planned a move to Texas, to our area. My heart felt as torn as my family: on one hand, I felt ecstatic that I would once again have someone to talk to; on the other hand, I could feel the oppression and enslavement that my life with him had brought about. I was scared that the secret would come out.

✢

The secret didn't feel right. The sale of the company continued moving ahead, the company did well, Thanksgiving 2004 came and went. The more I thought about the history of Auntie Anne's, the more strongly I felt I should tell my brothers and sisters about the sale agreement.

I thought of Aaron and Becky and how, as my very first employees, they played such a huge role in the early days. I thought of Fi and how supportive she'd always been through the years. I thought of Merrill and how, as director of franchising, he interviewed and brought in so many excellent franchisees. I thought of Dale, my brother and director of purchasing, and Jake, our VP of land development as well as my very first franchisee. Sure, Jonas and I owned Auntie Anne's the company, but there was a spirit about the place that couldn't be limited to shares—everyone who ever did anything to advance our company held emotional ownership.

Yet my advisors kept saying, "Wait." Finally I prayed.

"God, I feel terrible about not telling my brothers and sisters about the sale. I want to tell them. But I'm torn between what I feel is right and what everyone else is saying. I need a sign."

I thought for a moment. What would be a clear sign that I should tell them?

"Okay, God, if it's important for me to tell my brothers and sisters about the sale, have Sam Beiler call me and tell me he thinks I should tell them."

That was something I couldn't imagine happening, but within twenty-four hours he called.

"Anne? This is Sam. Hi. I've been thinking, and I know this hasn't been our approach so far, but I think that you should consider telling the siblings about the sale."

A few days later I found myself waiting in a small diner close to our head office. My coffee was hot, but outside the restaurant the December air was freezing cold. I had decided to meet with them one-on-one to tell them about my decision to sell the company to Sam. The first one would be there any minute.

❖

By the beginning of 1978, Pastor arrived in Texas, and my initial happiness at his arrival quickly turned to pain, mental anguish, and the guilt that only comes from keeping secrets. Once again I found myself drawn into a web of lies, secret rendezvous, sneaking here and there. Guilt. An overwhelming sense of confusion—if Pastor asked me to run away with him, would I? Could I leave Jonas and the children? I constantly thought about what I would need to pack if the opportunity presented itself.

This went on for three more years, nearly five years total from the months following Angie's death to the summer of 1981. But then, as soft as a gentle breeze, something began changing in me, something that yearned for the old days of simplicity. I wanted out of the pain and confusion. I finally realized that the pain I experienced by being with Pastor had to be worse than the pain I might feel if I left him. I began considering it in my mind, even talking to him about it.

"I'm not happy," I told him one day in a restaurant somewhere. "I'm not happy with the way I'm living."

"But you're happy when you're with me, right?" he would ask.

Most of the time, I thought to myself. *But not a genuine happiness, just a superficial kind of momentary happiness that comes and goes with my passing moods.*

There was another realization, though, that hurt me to the core and finally led me on the road to my freedom. I began realizing that Pastor was meeting other women, the same way he met with me. I started seeing his car parked at friends' houses or at places we would often meet. I began to realize that he lied to me all the time, manipulated me to no end.

At times I would see his car parked somewhere with one or the other of my sisters' cars. My breath would catch in my throat. *Surely not,* I thought to myself. *Surely not.* A feeling of overwhelming despair would rise in me. When I approached him about it, he would deny everything, but I started to see through his lies. I started to see the truth. He had been maintaining a relationship with both of my sisters the whole time, constantly driving a wedge deeper and deeper between us so that we would never find out, would never talk to each other about it, would never find freedom.

Finally the desire to be free of him became greater than my desire to be with him. I just wanted to be a happy wife and mother again. Then came the weekend I will never forget, the final push I needed to cut loose from Pastor. I remember one Saturday night suddenly feeling this urge to see my sister Fi, just to give her a hug. I so badly wanted to be close to her, the same way we were while growing up together. I thought back over the previous five years, how Pastor would make sure we couldn't spend time together.

I prayed to God, asking him to make it possible to sit beside Fi at church on Sunday morning. I thought that one small step would go a long way in healing our broken relationship. Sure enough, when Jonas, the girls, and I walked into church the next morning, there sat Fi with four empty seats beside her! I couldn't remember the last time she'd sat there with no one planted in the chair next to her. My heart kind of skipped a beat and I led the family down and took those four seats.

As I sat beside Fi, I felt comforted. She gave me her warmest smile and seemed glad that I chose to sit beside her. Then she put her arm around my shoulders and just gave me a squeeze. A simple act of kindness, but one that drove me to tears. I couldn't stop crying and tried to hide it from Fi, but she just held me tighter.

After church we talked for a little while, and I felt refreshingly alive. Then another surprise.

"Why don't you come over for coffee in the morning?" Fi asked.

I just nodded and could feel the tears of happiness rising again, but inside of me an excitement began to stir. I knew from years of random encounters that Monday morning was the time she spent with Pastor. If she was asking me to her house on a Monday morning . . . could that mean she had left him? I couldn't imagine.

The next morning I drove to her house fighting off the doubt and returning pessimism. So many times Becky and I or Fi and I planned to have coffee together, only for me to arrive and find they weren't home—later I would usually learn they had suddenly been called to the church by Pastor to help out with something. You cannot imagine my surprise when I came up the road and saw Fi's car in the driveway.

When she answered the door, the first words out of my mouth were full of shock.

"Aren't you supposed to be with Pastor this morning?" I asked, completely unable to rein in my curiosity.

That represented the first time we ever spoke of our encounters with him to one another. For five years the subject remained taboo, but suddenly the power of that secret was crumbling. Just mentioning the secret made me feel stronger, and I wondered if I might have the strength to start a new life free of him.

"I left him," she said simply. Suddenly an intense hope rose up in me—could I do that too? Could I regain a normal life? Could I be happy again?

Fi's encouragement over the next four months finally gave me the strength to do what I so badly wanted to do. So one morning I called Pastor and told him I needed to meet him at a restaurant for breakfast. While driving there I kept saying the words over and over again in my mind. "I don't want to see you anymore." But inside I still felt intense doubt regarding my ability to actually say those words to his face. I pulled into the parking space and looked up. He waved at me from inside. I got out of the car and walked to the door.

❖

December 2004. I sat in the diner waiting for the first meeting to begin. The lights weren't very bright, and I think it was one of those cold, cloudy winter days, so there wasn't much light coming in through the windows. I sat over a steaming cup of coffee, just reflecting on what I would say and wondering how my brothers and sisters would handle the news that I was selling the company.

That whole Christmas season nearly overcame me with its happiness, excitement for a new start, and also some sadness at the thought of selling Auntie Anne's after so many years. I couldn't help but think back over all of the things I had been through as a person, the obstacles we overcame as a company, the struggles and successes we experienced as a family. We had come so far in those twenty-five years, from being a totally broken family unit to being whole again, working together for nearly twenty years, spending holidays together, and going on family trips. Times were good again, and we functioned as a family should, mourning together in sad times and rejoicing together when good moments came along. The last thing I wanted was for the sale of Auntie Anne's to send us back into the dark ages again.

I was very nervous about telling them—the only thing we ever discussed with them regarding the sale of the company was that we were considering selling the company to my daughters or implementing an employee stock option plan. But as I met with each of them that day, I felt their support.

Most of them showed surprise at the timing as well as some disappointment that the company wouldn't be staying within the family. Yet most of them were also pleased the company wouldn't be sold to an outsider who most likely would have uprooted Auntie Anne's and attempted to integrate it into a larger corporation. One of them wished I would have discussed the possibility of selling the company to them. But at the end of each meeting, they all made one common point: they respected my decision to sell the company to Sam and were glad I told them.

As I got back into my car that afternoon, I felt weary from explaining myself over and over again, but also extremely relieved that the whole thing was over. As I drove home and the car began warming up, a sort of relaxation set in that only comes after a long-dreaded event has passed. Little did I know that the shock of the announcement would soon wear off and disappointment would set in. How could I know? My greatest concern at that time became telling my employees, an announcement I planned to make on January 4, just a few short weeks away.

❖

I walked into the restaurant in June 1981. Fi's encouragement had finally brought me to the place where I felt ready to leave Pastor. Finally inside, two conflicting feelings blasted me in the face: on one hand, I felt a physical relief at entering the coolness of the building (it was June in Texas, after all, and the weather was hot), but on the other hand, I felt the heat of anger rising up inside of me as soon as I saw him sitting at his table so nonchalantly.

I allowed him to steal so much from me, and during the last few weeks I'd begun realizing just how much of my life had been lost because of to his abuse of power during my time of vulnerability. I walked up to his table and sat down abruptly. I was on a roll and feeling determined, and the anger rising up inside of me gave me a special kind of courage. I had to tell him right away, get straight to the point.

"I'm not going to see you again," I said, speaking through a haze. The whole moment seemed like a dream, a moment I had relived so many times that when it actually took place, I couldn't believe my senses.

At first he tried to smooth-talk me, coming across as very forgiving and easygoing. He was a parent talking to an upset child, playing along for the moment, trying to get to the root of the problem in order to smooth things over. But that wasn't it. I wasn't momentarily upset with him—I was making a permanent decision, a life change, and nothing he could say would sweet-talk me into deciding any other way.

Finally he lost his patience.

"You can't make it without me," he said, almost sneering.

"We'll see," I said calmly. Inside I got angrier and angrier, but somehow I kept my cool.

I think he could tell that none of his approaches was working, and he simply said, "I'll run away with you. Come away with me. We'll leave everyone else and just go away, just the two of us."

I knew he was lying. He had strung me along for years with that promise. During the years after Angie's death, I'd felt so depressed that all I wanted to do was get away, and it was this constant promise of his to take me away from everything that was often the reason I stayed with him. When he told me there in that restaurant that he would run away with me, I did something I never even thought about doing, something I didn't even expect. I laughed in his face.

"No. I'm finished," I said.

I got up to leave.

"Let me tell you one more thing, then, if that's how you feel," he said slowly and with determination. I paused for a moment and looked at him just before turning away. He stared me right in the face and said something I have never forgotten.

"I will haunt you for the rest of your life."

I walked out to my car and drove away.

During the next few weeks and months, things were difficult. I still faced temptation, almost daily, to go back to him, to confide in him again. He called a few times, but after answering and hearing it was him, I never said a word. Sometimes I would listen to him talk, wanting to see him again. But I knew that if I met him again, I would just be going back to that old fear and sadness and slavery to an old secret. Eventually I learned to just hang up when he called.

For six months I rejoiced in the fact that I'd left him. I felt so free. As I look back on my life, I see now that those few months represented God sweeping into my life and literally tearing me from the jaws of evil. During those months God completely rescued me from a life of unhappiness and despair. It was as if I was just about to fall into a bottomless abyss when God came swooping down and carried me away on eagle's wings.

Not that the road back was easy. As I said, I faced many times of temptation. And now that I had recommitted myself to Jonas and the girls, there was a lot that we had to work through. At first I resolved not to tell Jonas—I thought it would just be too painful for him and for me: I was embarrassed by the deceptive life I'd lived, and I certainly didn't want to disappoint my two young daughters. But six months after I left Pastor, events began to turn, and suddenly I found myself in a position where I had to tell Jonas about my nearly six years of secrets.

❖

The emotional part of Auntie Anne's was hard to let go. You'd like to think that some things just last forever. But at the end of the day, I can't even accurately describe why I sold the company—the only thing I can say is that when it came to owning Auntie Anne's forever, well, it just wasn't meant to be.

It's not that I didn't feel qualified to own the company, inspire my employees, be the public face of Auntie Anne's, or influence the business world. I felt very comfortable in those roles. I think that sometimes God honors what we want in our lives, and maybe he knew that deep down I yearned for more time with my husband, with my girls, and with my grandchildren. But I also believe that God wanted me to step out in faith again with almost no knowledge of what lay ahead.

Just as God entrusted me with $6,000 back in 1988, so too did God entrust me with the sale of Auntie Anne's and millions of dollars. There was no particular reason that I started the first Auntie Anne's at Downingtown Farmers' Market apart from the fact that God put it in my path so I could support Jonas and his vision. I can say the same about the sale of the company. We are determined to be as faithful with the amount we received on selling Auntie Anne's as we were with that first $6,000 he blessed us with.

My seven-year-old grandson, Cristian, had an interesting take on the sale of the company. I was putting him to bed one night when he looked up at me.

"So, Nee Nee, I hear you're selling Auntie Anne's," he said, and tears welled up in his eyes, started rolling down his cheeks.

"Yeah," I said. "It's okay, Cristian."

He didn't agree.

"No, it's not okay!"

"Why?" I asked.

"Because," he said with a very troubled look on his face, "then you won't be the boss anymore."

"Well," I said, "that's all right. We're selling the company to Sam. You know Sam, and you know his kids."

For a moment that seemed to address his concerns. But only for a moment.

"Does that mean that Sam's picture is gonna be on the coupons now?"

"No," I said, trying not to smile. "We just felt like we needed to sell the company so that we would have more money to do what God wants us to do."

"But, Nee Nee. I thought you *had* a lot of money. I thought you *were* rich."

And with that he turned his head toward the wall beside his bed and wept. I put my arm around him, but he just shrugged me away.

I said, "Cristian, I am sorry that you feel so bad about it."

Then he turned to me and said, "Well, I don't care. I just don't like it."

I couldn't understand why he would care so much about our decision to sell the company. A few days later I told the story to my brother Dale, and we had a chuckle about Cristian's response.

"But that's exactly how I felt," Dale said. "I just don't like it."

Suddenly I appreciated Cristian's honesty. He didn't try to change my mind or make me feel bad for the decision I made. He didn't hide behind a bluff of anger or blame. His complete honesty about how he felt was so much easier for me to deal with, and so much healthier for him. He got mad, grieved, worked through it, and moved on. Meanwhile, the time came to tell the rest of the company.

January 4—time to tell the employees. I sat in that first conference room at 8:30 a.m., waited for the first group to show up. They filed in and sat around the boardroom table with me.

"I have an announcement to make, and I won't keep you guessing," I said. "I sold the company to Sam."

I stuck to a basic outline of points, trying to explain as best I could why I sold the company, why I thought Sam was the best buyer, what I looked forward to in life outside of Auntie Anne's. Toward the end of each meeting, I tried to rally everyone around Sam as the new leader. I wanted everyone to feel as good as I did about the sale, and even though I knew it wasn't possible, I did my best.

The support that I felt from my employees at Auntie Anne's completely overwhelmed me—nothing but positive support and incredible respect. I have dear, dear friends at the company, some of whom at that point I'd worked with for nearly eighteen years, so there was bound to be a few tears. The groups involved in operations were especially difficult to tell because for all of those years they represented my heart to the franchisees—perfect pretzels, clean stores, and friendly service. So many of them became as passionate as me when it came to upholding our high standards, and I greatly appreciated them during my years there.

Finally the day came to a close, and as I ushered the last group out of the conference room with hugs and good-byes, I felt mixed emotions. Relief that the day had ended and everyone knew my plans. An empty sort of finality that we were actually selling the company. Excitement for the new adventure, a new time in my life. And some sadness when I thought back on all the great memories, all the wonderful people, all the amazing experiences that I would not experience again.

I sat down in my office and took a deep breath, running

about an hour late for the final debrief with my siblings. When I finally walked into the room where they sat, I was shocked at the level of anxiety and tension in the air. After all of their initial support, after the immense support I felt from the employees, something changed. My siblings couldn't understand why they hadn't been included in the process and expressed their disappointment. I felt devastated and all I could say was , "I am sorry. I am sorry you feel this way." I left the building feeling that old familiar tug of depression and darkness wanting to pull me down.

It took me awhile to get over that feeling (I didn't leave my house for two days), but eventually I was able to sort through all the emotions and begin my new life. After all the negative things we had gone through as a family, still managing to come back together every time, this one last event was not going to divide us. Forgiveness is one of the most powerful forces in the world, able to completely turn the tide of events.

❖

I sat staring at the phone with determination. December in Texas was about as cold as it got, and sometimes if we got a frost on the ground, my mind would go back to Pennsylvania and my family and Angie. But at that moment I wasn't thinking about Pennsylvania. I was thinking about Pastor's wife.

At that point, in the winter of 1981, I had been free of Pastor for over six months. I felt a freedom I barely recognized. Happiness came back slowly, one notch at a time, but I made progress. Then suddenly the rumors started to fly around the church, the same rumors we heard when we were back home at our church. Pastor was doing this, Pastor was involved with that—and finally Jonas; Fi's husband, Mike, and Becky's husband, Aaron, started to wonder. What was going on? Could it be that the trouble hounding Pastor from church to church was of his own making? Were the rumors true?

Something came over me in those days, a feeling of terrible remorse for what I did during those six years. For some reason I felt compelled to apologize to Pastor's wife for the things I did—my conscious wouldn't let me off the hook. This feeling of remorse is what led me to that moment, that sitting by the phone waiting for the strength to make the call.

Finally the strength came.

"Hello?" she answered.

I knew she'd heard the rumors. I knew the whispers of his infidelity had reached her ears. I explained to her that the things she had heard were true, and finally I told her that I was one of those women.

Silence.

"Have you told Jonas?" she asked me.

I felt as though she'd kicked me in the stomach: the wind went out of me, and a startled feeling crept up from my insides.

"No," I said slowly. The notion of telling Jonas pressed in on me in those days, but I didn't want to do anything to break our happiness—I carried it around like a glass bubble, protecting it from anything and everything. Telling Jonas would be like throwing that bubble up in the air, to him, and praying he could catch it.

"No," I repeated, "I haven't told Jonas."

"Are you planning to?"

"No, I wasn't planning to."

"Well," she said evenly but without malice, "if you don't, I will."

"Oh," I said, trying to sound calm. "Then I'll tell him. I'd rather tell him myself."

I hung up.

For a moment I sat there, not knowing what to say or do. "If you don't tell him, I will." That sentence just kept ringing through my mind, and suddenly one thought took precedence: I had to tell Jonas, and immediately. No one else could tell him that horrible secret before I did. He had to hear it from me. I drove straight to his body shop, and when I got there, he was coming out of his office.

"Hey," he said. "What are you doing here?"

"Hi. Jonas? You know those things you've been hearing about all those women with Pastor?"

He nodded.

"I was one of those women."

A look came over Jonas's face that I'd never seen before, a look of intense hurt and surprise and shock. I couldn't bear to look at it. It wasn't rage or anger but more along the lines of deep disappointment and confusion. Yet even those words cannot adequately describe the look on his face. And suddenly all of the guilt came rushing back. What had I done?

"I'm sorry. And I'm a sorry person." I choked the words out amid rising sobs.

I didn't touch him or walk up to him. I just blurted out those words through the tears that were coming, then turned and left because I could not look at his face, in his eyes. I ran from that look, went to work. During my lunch break I tried to call him three or four times. No one answered. The look on his face had been filled with such despair that I couldn't imagine what he might do.

Finally I got home, and he wasn't there. I started panicking:

Where would he be? Who should I call? Just when the fear rose and threatened to suffocate me, I heard his car pull into the driveway. Relief.

He came in the door.

"Honey, we need to talk. We need to talk," he said.

"About what?" I asked. About what? What a stupid thing to say! My state of mind at that time was completely short circuited. I felt that I had said all there was to say, and I didn't want to talk about it anymore, especially with Jonas.

"We have to talk," he said again. "But we'll wait until the girls are in bed tonight."

I felt more nervous than ever but went through my daily routine, preparing dinner and getting the girls to bed. Was he going to kick me out of the house? I had nowhere to go. Was he going to leave me? I couldn't blame him if he did.

Jonas worked out in his shed most of the afternoon and evening. I can only imagine the thoughts that raced through his head as he spent time out there alone. The night came all too quickly for my liking, and soon we stood across from one another in the kitchen. I didn't want the discussion to go on for too long, and I figured if we stood up, it wouldn't, so I leaned against the kitchen counter. Time to talk.

Jonas broke the silence first.

"It's not so much that we have to talk about this issue," he said slowly, deliberately. "It's more that I have something I want to say to you."

"Oh," I said uncertainly. I expected anger. I expected accusations. And if Jonas wanted to say something, I thought he had that right, especially after what I'd done. But I didn't think I could take any verbal beatings at that point. I had been tearing myself down for years, and I just wasn't in any sort of state to handle heavy criticism. I knew I deserved it, but I couldn't have handled it.

Jonas continued.

"I just want to tell you that I want you to be happy. If you want to leave me, then just promise me one thing. Can you do that?"

"I don't know if I can," I said, amazed that he still concerned himself with my happiness. "I've broken many promises."

"Well," he said, "just promise me that you won't leave me in the middle of the night with a note on my dresser."

"Okay," I said. The tears started to well up in my eyes, and I hoped he was nearly finished, because I didn't want to lose it in front of him. But he pressed on.

"If you decide to leave, just tell me about it. I'll help you pack. I just want you to promise you'll take the girls with you, because they need their mother."

Forgiveness can take your breath away.

If Jonas had accused me at that moment, I would have run. Even though I had nowhere else to go, home still felt like the last safe haven, and if he would have charged me, I would have been forced out. Don't get me wrong—at that time I thought I deserved to be accused! But it would have pushed me away.

Instead, Jonas's words made me feel safe, made me feel valued in an area of my life where I had always felt weak: my mothering. Nowhere else in the world offered a place for me at that moment in my life, yet Jonas told me I was valued. I was a good mother. He didn't want me to leave.

Forgiveness took my breath away.

CHAPTER TWELVE

Enlarging the Future

Forgiveness does not change the past, but it does enlarge the future.

—PAUL BOESE

There are a few times in our lives when pure, unadulterated evil shows itself—most of the time evil works its ways much more subtly. Yet those moments come once every so often, and what we are confronted with is pure fear, hatred, and destruction. Usually the temptation during these times is to run away, to shrink back, to retreat into a dark hole until the time passes. Our initial reaction is usually not forgiveness.

Even as I write this final chapter in my story, only a few weeks have passed since pure evil tried to shatter a small town. The story began with a family man, a hard worker by all accounts, a husband, the father of small children (in other words, someone who appeared to be entirely normal), yet he made horrible plans and carried them out, walking into a small Amish schoolhouse not five miles from my house and shooting ten small girls. Five of them were killed, two of them sisters, ages seven and eight.

Yet in the face of such evil and hatred, the Amish community's first reaction was one of forgiveness! CNN reported that a grandfather of one of the murdered Amish girls said of the killer on the day of the murder: "We must not think evil of this man." A member of the Brethren community living near the Amish in Lancaster County explained: "I don't think there's anybody here that wants to do anything but forgive, and not only reach out to those who have suffered a loss in that way but to reach out to the family of the man who committed these acts."

In fact, that's exactly what happened: the Amish reportedly set up a fund for donations to go to the family of the man who shot their children; the Amish families invited that same family to one of the funerals, normally a private affair to which very few non-Amish are ever invited; there is even the story of one of the local Amish preachers finding the shooter's wife and father-in-law, telling them he did not hold them responsible. He hugged them and they held each other, the three of them, weeping.

There will be no lawsuits. There will be no public statements of sadness. There will be no press conferences casting doubt on the performance of the police or the emergency services or the government. There will be only forgiveness.

That is not to say there will be no suffering. Do the families mourn for the children? Of course they do. Do the mothers feel sadness, loss? They must. Does the father of those two small girls buried side by side wake up in the morning and miss his little children? Of course he does. But when evil rose up in that small town and carried out its horrible atrocities, these families, this community, all of us in fact, were presented with a stark choice: do we react out of fear and hatred and allow evil to perpetuate its destructive self, or do we choose to allow the healing process to begin?

Forgiveness continues its healing process in our small town, something that began only a few hours after the event took place. A few short days later, I drove on some back roads close to the school where the shooting occurred. I approached a stop sign where I had to turn right or left. But then I paused—in front of me was a dirt lane that led back to another Amish school. *How do they do it?* I thought to myself. *How do they go right back to school?* That's when I noticed: both the gate to the drive and the doors of the schoolhouse were flung wide open. They would not let hatred force them into a dark place of seclusion and fear. Their response to the atrocity was to open wide the doors.

Forgiveness also continues its healing process in my life. As others showed me love and encouragement and forgiveness, my life began gaining strength. I know of no other more powerful life force than forgiveness. When speaking about it, my husband loves to bring up the old Sunday school adage: forgive and forget. "Impossible," he says. Forgive and forget is a saying we simply cannot apply to those events in our lives that most need forgiveness—usually these are events that have changed us, events we will never forget. Instead, Jonas adheres to another saying he has heard my sister Fi say: "Forgive because you *cannot* forget."

When my extended family found out about the abusive situation that had occurred between Pastor and me, their initial reaction could have been one of disgust or surprise or, more appropriate to our conservative background, shame. They could have let me slip off the family radar; after all, we lived so far away that they easily could have just written me off.

Yet they chose grace and forgiveness. I informed my brothers of everything through a letter and waited for the fallout. You cannot imagine the roller coaster of emotions I felt when my oldest brother, Jake, and his wife showed up unexpectedly at our church one Sunday morning in 1982. He drove all those hundreds of miles from Pennsylvania to Texas just to be there with me, to show me his support, to tell me he loved me. I felt totally overwhelmed and forgiven!

"What are you guys doing here?" I asked, amazed.

"We just wanted to support you," Jake said in his typically quiet way when talking about serious things. Jake would be the one to come by Downingtown over five years later on one of my first weekends as owner, just to offer the same encouragement and support. One by one my family members began showing me their love and forgiveness through letters or phone calls or visits. This amazing grace allowed me to continue my journey back to happiness and some sense of a normal life after six years of darkness and confusion.

❖

My mom and dad also pounced on the opportunity to show me their love and support. Even during my dark years, they came down every winter for a month or so just to see how we were doing—they would pull a camper down and live in our driveway. Even though we'd rejected them so coldly when we left Pennsylvania, they kept trying to break down those walls, slowly picking away.

About a year after freedom returned into my life, doctors discovered that Dad needed open-heart surgery, so Becky, Fi, and I decided to drive from Texas to Pennsylvania to be there for the operation. Covering all of those miles together felt very therapeutic to me: the three of us girls were back together again, the first time in years! I thought about so much during that trek north, but I felt especially hopeful that I would get to talk to Dad about my abuse and apologize for not believing him when it came to Pastor.

Fi, Becky, and I hung out at the hospital for a week along with our brothers and in-laws, and it became a time of healing for our relationship. Daddy recovered from his surgery, but the opportunity never came up for me to tell him face-to-face about what I had gone through. I wasn't too disappointed, though, just because of how well our family seemed to be healing. I never thought it would be possible, but suddenly we were supporting each other again, loving one another, staying in touch.

Dad recovered from his surgery, and the next winter he and Mom came down to see us again. At that point I still didn't talk about my dark years with anyone—I felt that I had dealt with the situation and the time had come to move on. I guess I didn't realize how many other issues still remained. But in any case, that winter was the best winter we had with my parents.

One day Dad came to see me at work—I worked at a steak-house from 11:00 a.m. to 2:00 p.m. on most afternoons just to make a little extra money. When I got off work, I sat down with Dad at the far booth next to a window that looked out onto the street. That was the first time I ever remember spending one-on-one time with Dad—when you are part of a family with eight children, very few people get the chance to be alone with Dad! I felt special that day in the restaurant, just him and I talking together.

I also remember feeling like he was my daddy again, feeling that for some reason our father-daughter relationship was being restored. He never showed a lot of affection while we were growing up, but sitting there with him made me feel like a little girl again. It reminded me of the feeling I used to get when I was young and we would be driving to market—I always wanted to perch on that middle seat right beside him.

Sitting there with him, I wanted to tell him everything. I wanted to tell him that he had been right all along, I wanted to say sorry for all of the small injustices I had done him, I wanted to tell him I loved him so much. I wanted to tell him everything I had been through. But I couldn't find the words.

In his own way, he talked around the subject, sometimes darting in terribly close to the unspoken things, then easing away. We didn't talk directly about my past, but he said enough to bring peace to my heart. I could tell he knew about what had happened, and he still loved me. I knew I was forgiven.

As we got up to leave, I smiled. I felt grateful we'd had that time together, even if I hadn't been able to verbalize all the things I had been through. As we walked out of the restaurant, Dad turned to me and grinned.

"I love you, Anne," he said.

Now, I always knew my parents loved me. But in our culture we didn't say it much, and that is the only time I remember my dad ever saying it to me like that. He couldn't have said it at a better time.

After Daddy left the restaurant that day, he went to Jonas's shop to have something on his car fixed. He and Mom were getting ready to drive to Atlanta for a quilt show. Jonas fixed whatever it was that needed to be fixed, so they packed up and left, their small trailer in tow. Less than a week later we got a call from Mom—she was in Atlanta.

"Anne, Dad fell over again, like he did before, and we're in the hospital," she said in a hollow voice.

"What?" I asked, shocked, looking at the clock—it was after 8:00 p.m. He had been fine the other day at the restaurant. "We'll leave right away—we can be there in around twelve hours."

"No, no. The doctors say he will be okay. Don't drive through the night; just come in the morning."

"Is he conscious?" I asked.

"No, well, he's kind of in and out right now."

"What? What do you mean in and out? Are you sure he's going to be okay?"

"They're saying he'll be all right in the morning."

So we made plans for the children and decided to leave in the morning. Carl, my youngest brother and future president of Auntie Anne's, was visiting us and wanted to drive to the hospital in Atlanta with the three of us sisters.

But before we could even get out the door in the morning, Mom called again.

"Daddy's dying," she said in a choked voice.

"What do you mean?" I asked, panic filling my voice.

"The doctors didn't realize it, but he has been hemorrhaging in his head through the night. He doesn't have long."

We left right away and proceeded to get a speeding ticket in every state from Texas to Georgia. The first cop who pulled us over said he would radio ahead. I guess that didn't happen, because each time we got pulled over, no one knew what we were talking about. We raced along in that little brown Toyota station wagon, and it shimmied the whole way, shaking back and forth as soon as we got up over 55 miles per hour.

Every two hours we stopped for gas and called Mom to see how Daddy was doing.

"He's not getting better," she'd say. By the sound of her voice, she wasn't doing very well, either.

"Mom, tell him we're coming."

"I'm not in the room with him," she said quietly. "I feel so alone, and I don't know what to do."

When we got to the hospital, we raced inside. But he was gone. He'd died an hour before we got there, and we were devastated. Shocked. An awful numbness began setting in. Why hadn't we come last night? Why hadn't we gone faster? Why didn't we leave earlier that morning? Why did Daddy have to die alone in a room in that strange hospital in a faraway city?

We all decided to just continue driving up to Pennsylvania for the funeral. Eventually everyone got there—we three sisters and Carl arrived from Atlanta, the rest of our families from Texas, and the three brothers who had been desperately driving from Pennsylvania to Atlanta, trying to get there before Daddy died.

We got to Mom and Dad's house in Lancaster County around 11:30 that night. Mom's sisters were all there, and they made dinner for us. We shared that meal together in a bonding sort of sadness, finished eating just after midnight, and then tried to get some sleep. For those who couldn't sleep, there were extended family members visiting throughout the night, and I was reminded of how strong the family bonds were in our hometown. I felt such good closure just being there, having family around us, supporting us. And I felt very blessed to have had that time with Daddy at the steakhouse.

We buried Daddy right beside Angie. The cold felt bitter, and it was raining or sleeting or something wet and miserable. It was the first time we were all together in seven years, the first time since we had that blowup in Mom and Dad's house with Pastor parked in the driveway. Our togetherness at that point brought me great hope for the future, even amid the sadness that came with Daddy's passing.

I thought of our last meeting, and I felt so glad to know that he still loved me and forgave me. We all sang together the same song we'd sung at Angie's burial: "Daddy won't have to worry anymore."

Daddy's funeral represented many things to me and helped bring about a healing in our family that could have taken much longer. That togetherness also helped me to realize that I was truly forgiven—the more time we spent together, the more comfortable and accepted I felt because no one was condemning me; no one was trying to make me feel bad for my past.

But there was still one person who didn't forgive me. One person who held me responsible for everything that had happened, one person who continued insisting that I would have to pay for everything I'd done. I couldn't argue with that person, at least not successfully, and no matter what I did, I couldn't get that person to stop whispering to me, "You are a failure, you are a bad person, you have been a terrible mother."

Of course, that person was me. I was the only person who refused to forgive.

And then another funeral. Another passing. And another revelation.

1995, 1996, 1997—those years challenged me as I tried to cope with a company expanding at an unbelievable rate, the guilt of my past, and two daughters with so many issues of their own for which I felt responsible. At the root of my insecurity was my relationship with them—I often felt that if only I would have been a better mother during their early years, perhaps they would not have gotten involved in the trouble they did. I felt like a complete failure and couldn't even remember those years in the late '70s and early '80s. Those were such formative years for my little girls, and I couldn't remember anything about them. But then God decided it was time for me to begin the final process of forgiving myself.

Jonas's mother passed away in May 1998, the end of a long, long journey for her. There was the viewing, then the funeral, and after it all we came together as a family and supported one another. During the following days we would often congregate at Jonas's father's house, just hanging out with whoever came by, looking through his mother's old things and reminiscing.

One day we went into her room to clean up and sort through some of the things that Jonas's father wanted to give to the children. I opened a drawer and found a couple of boxes, the white, very thin cardboard clothing boxes used to gift-wrap things. When I opened the boxes, I found envelopes absolutely stuffed full, some nearly bursting. I pulled the boxes out onto her bed and looked a little closer.

The envelopes each had a year, or time period, written on the front in her handwriting, and as I started looking through them, I realized she had kept every single letter I wrote while we lived in Texas! All of the Christmas cards, birthday cards, letters from the girls, letters from me—everything sat there in those boxes.

"Dear Mom and Pop," they all began, "greetings of love from all of us."

"TO GRUSSMUMMY," began a small plain postcard in a child's all-capital writing, "HI. I LOVE YOU. HOW ARE YOU FEELING? I LIKE TEXAS. LAWONNA LYN."

"Tell Grussdaddy," said another one, "that I said hi. We like Texas. I love you."

"On Tuesday," I wrote in a letter dated October 25, 1977, "I made some soft sugar cookies and by the time I was finished I didn't have many left. LaWonna was delivering cookies to all the neighbors and she was enjoying every minute of it. I was happy cause she was so happy giving those cookies away . . . She found some friends across the road that she plays with quite a bit . . ."

"LaVale is doing okay," I wrote in another letter, "as active as ever and cute as a button these days. She is starting to say a lot of words and an awful lot of jabbering. LaWonna is doing fine and still loves school. It's only four weeks until Christmas . . ."

"I got LaVale off the bottle and she didn't hardly even miss it! I am so thankful. LaWonna was in a Christmas parade down here. She belongs to a group called the Bluebirds and their group marched in the parade. She was so tickled to be able to do that . . ."

"To Grusmommy, I love you. I am Getting Me ShotS On TueSday—Thank You For all The letters. LaWonna."

And then in the early '80s LaVale's little letters started showing up.

"Dear Grussmommy, I'm at Loyd's now and I'm sick with Viruse. How are you? I'm fine now. Have you been sick? What is Grussdouty doing? I'm hoping to get a letter from you. Love you. From LaVale."

The letters went on and on, each one a snapshot of the years my mind had blocked out, so many little reminders that I'd been a good mother to my girls during those years, even when I had felt terrible about myself. I read through those letters and began to feel something changing inside of me. I didn't recognize it at the time, but I was finding the grace to forgive myself.

✤

I've seen forgiveness complete its healing work in the lives of my husband, Jonas, and our two daughters, LaWonna and LaVale. Both of our girls have discovered the power of grace and forgiveness through their own experiences with abuse. Despite all they went through when their innocence was taken away from them as children, the choices they made as a result of their pain and anger caused them to become women of great compassion. They don't see themselves as victims but rather as conquorers, and they live their lives with purpose and meaning. Moreover, their experiences have given them an exceptional ability to forgive.

LaVale is the proud mom of Cristian, the little boy who was so honest with me about his unhappiness when I sold Auntie Anne's. He is the love of her life and was our first grandchild. Cristian is a gift to our family. LaVale decided to further her education and is going to college to get her degree. God has redeemed her from a life of self-destruction, and she has discovered that God is in her corner and has a plan for her life. She has a passion to help those who have been used and abused and wants to make a difference in her world.

LaWonna also worked through her abuse and is not only a survivor but truly an overcomer. She now has a family of her own and lives a very full life with her husband, Russ, and their three children, Trinity, Ryan, and Mia. She has the capacity to be compassionate toward those who are suffering with issues of abuse. She loves deeply and forgives quickly.

❖

During my years at Auntie Anne's, when I started to slip back into feelings of guilt and depression and hopelessness, I bought a condo in Sarasota. I needed a place to escape to, a place where I could get away from the business and the worries and even my own family at times. Ironically, that place that gave me the isolation I craved has turned into a meeting place where every other year all of my brothers and sisters and all of our husbands and wives, as well as my mother, converge for a time just to hang out.

Sixteen of us, all sharing the common bonds of family, all having at some time or other worked at Auntie Anne's or owned an Auntie Anne's location. They say you should never work with family. Well, I can't say we didn't have our share of major disagreements and painful arguments. I can't say we never hurt each other with our words or decisions, because we did, sometimes in a big way that left loads of frustration and disappointment in its wake. But I can say that we still get together every month for a sibling meeting and share our lives. I can say we take trips together and laugh until our bellies ache. I can say that we still support each other through everything. What else needs to be said?

About a year ago I went down to the condo to start this book, and at some point I found myself just walking the beach. The sun was almost invisible behind low gray clouds, and a strong wind whipped up the sand so it stung my legs and sometimes even my face. I carried my sandals, walking barefoot, leaning forward into the wind. Thinking back on my life, the twists and turns it had taken, I felt truly amazed that I was whole. Sometimes even now I cannot believe how high the highs were, or how low the lows—emotionally I went to the very brink of hell and back and felt the forces of evil pulling me, trying to force me over the edge, almost to the point of suicide. Yet somehow I am now thrilled to live this life, feeling that each day is one to be enjoyed. I feel like a new person.

God's grace and forgiveness are what got me through it all. Today when I think about forgiveness, I wonder, *Have I forgiven others as I have been forgiven?* Sometimes my old hurts begin to throb and I feel the emotions of anger and depression. It's during these moments that I think about Jesus and what he said while dying on the cross surrounded by his accusers and executioners. "Father, forgive them."

This statement has become a lifestyle for me, and the benefit is a life of joy. Many times I even feel happy because I know now that "life is hard but God is good," and I try not to confuse the two. Happiness is a choice I can make when life is hard, but the joy I have in my soul is permanent.

I have been forgiven much. In the past I would go to Angie's grave and flash back to the pain and grief of her death and the life I was trapped in. I would feel paralyzed with anxiety and pain. Today when I visit her grave, I think back to my past and realize that the path I travelled made me who I am. I know I have conquered and I am free at last! I no longer feel the need to even the score or get revenge.

Forgiveness has transformed me: each time I visit Angie, I feel more and more at peace, appreciating the life God brought me through. Now I understand that "out of my pain, my passion was born." Redemption could only complete its work when I began to forgive.

To describe the power of forgiveness and its effects on my life would require a book of its own, yet even then I couldn't cover everything that forgiveness has done in my life. To forgive, and be forgiven, has given me the kind of life that I never could have imagined or thought was possible this side of heaven. Forgiveness has become my lifestyle, and the benefits for this life are many: health, happiness, and peace of mind, to name just a few.

There was a time when I thought I could never experience a healthy, happy marriage, but I have that now. There was a time when the idea of having fulfilling relationships with my daughters seemed impossible, but the three of us have never been closer. Confession, forgiveness, and a willingness to sort through my story gave me the keys to unlocking my past, giving me hope for my future with those I love most: my family.

As I stood in the wind and heard the waves that day in Florida, I reflected on my past, amazed at how different I felt compared to my first few visits to that beach in 1995. The waves crashed. The ocean stretched out farther than I could see, immense and unstoppable. I thought about how much bigger that ocean was than me and how, if I let it, it could just sweep right over me and carry me away. If I just threw myself in, I would not be able to resist it.

God's forgiveness is an ocean.

Acknowledgments

Writing a book has been a dream since 1975 when our daughter Angela took her flight to heaven. I suppose most of us think of writing a book after we experience tragedy or traumatic events that alter the path we are on. Disappointments in life make us or break us, and if it wasn't for the love and support I have received through the years, I would have become broken beyond repair. I wrote this book for people who need hope, and I pray you have found it in the pages of my story.

I have been forgiven "seventy times seven" by a loving God, my husband, my children, and my friends. Because I have been forgiven, I have been able to forgive those who hurt me. It has been a very long journey, but experiencing forgiveness has given me great peace.

I owe my gratitude to a number of people, but first and foremost I will say that the grace and love of my heavenly Father have sustained me. He has given me faith and courage when I thought I couldn't face another day. He has redeemed me and made my life more than I ever dreamed was possible! To him I say, "Thank you."

My family, what can I say? My dear husband, Jonas, has been

my rock and was the one person in my life who loved me uncon-ditionally. He was the man who loved me in a way that all of us want to be loved. Through all of my sin, despair, and depression he stayed with me; and quietly, day in and day out, year after year, he stayed committed to our family. Words of gratitude are difficult to express and I simply say, "I respect you, dear, and thank you."

My three daughters are a constant reminder of the miracle of life, and to be a mother is my highest calling in this life. You are a precious and priceless gift to me. Angela is the one among us who has "arrived." It is because of her short life of less than two years that I have experienced the depth and height of sadness and joy. I believe she has prayed many per-fect prayers for me and my family and stands among the great-est as fulfilling her purpose for this life. "A little child will lead them" (Isaiah 11:6 NLT). Her life here on earth and in heaven is a strong influence for us to fulfill our purpose while we travel planet Earth and then to join her where she lives. Angela, you are my traveling buddy, my "Angel."

LaWonna Lyn, our firstborn, and Joy LaVale, our third and youngest, are a constant source of support, love, and encourage-ment. Through the years you have been directly impacted by all my "craziness." You have had your own struggles as you watched and experienced the lies and deceits that were unspo-ken yet very real in our home. You have experienced the death and resurrection of our family, and through it all you have given me not what I deserved, but what I needed, love and grace. You have seen the power of God as he has kept us and never let us go. I love you more than life, and you both are "so beautiful to me." You gave me a reason to stay when I wanted to run; I had to be with you, and today I am. All the pain and frustration couldn't separate us, and it's because you loved me and I loved you. Love is a powerful force, and where love is miracles happen. I am a proud mom, and I see God in you every day.

Russ, my son-in-law. You bring laughter and life to us on a daily basis. Thank you for the three beautiful grandchildren you have blessed us with: Trinity, Ryan, and Mia. They are the joy of my life.

Cristian, my oldest grandson. You came into our lives when we needed a baby to hold, and you are a "little man of integrity." I am proud of you.

My mom, who at the age of eighty-seven, still wants to do things for me. She is always available to help anytime I ask. Thank you for allowing me to be in your kitchen when I was a little girl. You never complained when it got messy.

I have five brothers and two sisters who have loved, accepted, and supported me in unbelievable ways. Their tolerance and love for me can only be described as "It's just what families do." They have been kind and loved me since I was a little girl on the farm, and that same love and support has carried me through Auntie Anne's and beyond.

Jake, the oldest. Thank you for coming all the way to Texas during one of the darkest days of my life just to support me and later to become one of the team at Auntie Anne's. You were also one of our first franchisees.

Sam, better known to us as "Chub." Thank you for being the first one to connect with me after six long years of silence. I wanted to end it all. You said you would call me once a week until I was doing better, and you did.

Dale. You left your secure job and plunged into Auntie Anne's as the "warehouse guy." You did anything that was needed to meet our ever-growing warehouse needs. Today you are still at Auntie Anne's managing a multimillion-dollar warehouse. You're like the Energizer bunny. Thank you.

Merrill, you were our very first "delivery boy" at Auntie Anne's and one of our first franchisees. Those were the days, right? Through the years you have been my inspiration, my encourager, and now my pastor. Thank you.

Carl. You came knocking on my door when you saw the need and opportunity. I'll never forget the answer to prayer you were to me. You took what was already successful and laid a strong foundation for the future of Auntie Anne's. You put systems in place that helped us grow and took the company worldwide in less than five years. What a ride! Thank you.

My two sisters, Becky and Fi. We have been through more together than we can talk about at times, yet we have this silent connection that only sisters can have. Thanks for the victories that we have experienced together and for staying when you wanted to run. Thanks for being there for me when I thought it was over for us. There were times when I thought we would never speak to each other again, yet somehow we did the impossible: We overcame our hurt and anger. We spoke to each other and we hugged. After all, we are attached at the hip.

When God gave me my two sisters, he gave me two blessings that he knew I needed in the good times and in the bad. When we were little girls, we would snuggle in the one bed we slept in during the cold, hard winters. As an adult I feel us snuggling emotionally in the cold, harsh realities of life. Thank you.

To be your sister is God's gift to me, and he knew I would need your friendship, strength, and love in my adult years. Without you I would never have been able to grow Auntie

Anne's in the early years. God is keeping score, and he will bless you in this life and in the life to come.

Thanks to all my family. You are incredibly hardworking and kind! We also have more fun than a barrel of monkeys when we get together the first Monday of each month.

There are many more family members, including many nieces and nephews, who made Auntie Anne's successful.

My sister-in-law Ruth was with me from day one and is still with the company today. You are amazing.

My brother-in-law Aaron was the first risk taker. You left your job and came to help us. You did whatever it took to get the job done, and I am grateful for the many long days and nights you gave to the start and growth of the company. Your constant hard work and sacrifice were an example to all who followed you.

My sister-in-law Vern. Thanks for listening to me when I was angry and depressed and wanted to run away.

Pop Beiler. Thank you for giving me an opportunity of a lifetime by giving me $6,000 to start our little pretzel stand at Downingtown Farmers' Market. You gave me the money and trusted me to fully repay you when I could. Your trust was a real encouragement, because we were completely broke and had no way of knowing if I could ever pay you back. That gift set us on a path that will take a lifetime to appreciate.

Shawn Smucker, my nephew and the one who was my shadow as we wrote my story together. You were an answer to prayer the day we had coffee together. The project was a pleasure because of your gift of writing, your kindness, and your encouragement. Thank you.

There are three other men I want to thank because they restored my trust.

Tom Wilson, my first pastor after my time of deep mistrust in God, church, and pastors. You welcomed our family with loving arms. Our friendship is a reminder of God's grace.

Omar Beiler, my pastor at the time when we were a start-up company. You spoke into my life when I thought I had gone as far as I could possibly go with fifty stores. You said I could keep going if I would gather people around me to do what I couldn't do. You were right, and I found scores of people who knew a whole lot more than I did, and what a gift they were to me.

Dr. Richard Dobbins. You saved my life from complete destruction, emotionally and spiritually, by your wisdom and understanding of my behavior. You provided a safe place for me to spill my guts and gave me a better theological understanding of life.

Sam Beiler, my successor at Auntie Anne's. You understood my vision and purpose and stayed the course for nearly sixteen years. In the end I knew you were the man for the future growth of Auntie Anne's because you are a man of wisdom.

Elli Zeamer. My first assistant, who came to me as a total stranger and asked if I needed an assistant. I wasn't looking and had no clue that I was in desperate need of one. Thanks you for assisting me in many ways in the early years of Auntie Anne's.

Dave Hood. Thank you for coming all the way from Chicago to Amish Country. Your experience in the world of franchising was a gift to our fledgling company,

Mary Lou Frisbie. Thank you for serving me well for twelve years. You've kept me and my family going in the right direction, always being in the right place at the right time. I would have lost my way without you.

All the employees at Auntie Anne's. It is your enthusiasm and love for the company and the product that gave me joy each day. You are the reason that I am blessed and able to write this book. My story would not have the same ending if it wasn't for the success of Auntie Anne's. Your love and loyalty is amazing to me. I will never forget you!

The franchisees are a group of people who have been a surprise and blessing to me. Your trust in me and the product in the beginning astounded me. You came to us from all over the world and wanted to sell pretzels. What a simple concept and what trust you had! I was a simple farm girl with no experience; you knew that and trusted me anyway. What a ride we had together!

Thank you to another group of people who "brought a song" into my life again, the Gaither Homecoming Friends. You bless my life and make my spirit soar each time I listen to you sing. Your songs continue to help me get through any circumstance I may encounter as I journey on.

Thank you, Wes, my agent, for being my guide and source of information. Thank you for your great patience and for helping me stay on track with this project.

Thank you to all those at Thomas Nelson who believed in this project.

There are many others who have touched my life and connected with me at just the right place and time. Thank you for your encouragement—spiritually, professionally, and personally.

Printed in the USA
CPSIA information can be obtained
at www.ICGtesting.com
LVHW051532210724
785408LV00008B/82